Picturebooks

The picturebook is now recognized as a sophisticated art form that has provided a space for some of the most exciting innovations in the field of children's literature. This book brings together the work of expert scholars from the UK, the USA and Europe to present original theoretical perspectives and new research on picturebooks and their readers.

The authors draw on a variety of disciplines such as art and cultural history, semiotics, philosophy, cultural geography, visual literacy, education and literary theory in order to revisit the question of what a picturebook is, and how the best authors and illustrators meet and exceed artistic, narrative and cultural expectations. The book looks at the socio-historical conditions of different times and countries in which a range of picturebooks have been created, pointing out variations but also highlighting commonalities. It also discusses what the stretching of borders may mean for new generations of readers, and what contemporary children themselves have to say about picturebooks.

This book is based on a special issue of the *New Review of Children's Literature and Librarianship*.

Evelyn Arizpe is Senior Lecturer in the School of Education at the University of Glasgow, UK, and coordinates the MEd in Children's Literature and Literacies. She has taught and published widely in the areas of literacies, reader-response to picturebooks and children's literature. Previous publications include *Children Reading Picture: Interpreting visual texts* (2003).

Maureen Farrell is Senior Lecturer in the Language Department of the School of Education at the University of Glasgow, UK. Her research interests focus around Scottish Children's and Young Adult literature, picturebooks and identity formation. She has published several articles on these topics.

Julie McAdam is a teacher educator in the Language Department of the School of Education at the University of Glasgow, UK. Prior to working at Glasgow, Julie worked in Cairo, Budapest, Lisbon and the United Arab Emirates in EFL. She was a contributing author to *Threshold Concepts in the Disciplines* (2009).

Picturebooks

Beyond the Borders of Art, Narrative and Culture

Edited by
**Evelyn Arizpe, Maureen Farrell and
Julie McAdam**

Routledge
Taylor & Francis Group

LONDON AND NEW YORK

First published 2013
by Routledge
2 Park Square, Milton Park, Abingdon, Oxon, OX14 4RN

Simultaneously published in the USA and Canada
by Routledge
711 Third Avenue, New York, NY 10017

Routledge is an imprint of the Taylor & Francis Group, an informa business

This book is a reproduction of the *New Review of Children's Literature and Librarianship*, volume 17, issue 2. The Publisher requests to those authors who may be citing this book to state, also, the bibliographical details of the special issue on which the book was based.

British Library Cataloguing in Publication Data
A catalogue record for this book is available from the British Library

ISBN13: 978-0-415-81418-8

Typeset in Baskerville
by Taylor & Francis Books

Publisher's Note
The publisher would like to make readers aware that the chapters in this book may be referred to as articles as they are identical to the articles published in the special issue. The publisher accepts responsibility for any inconsistencies that may have arisen in the course of preparing this volume for print.

Contents

Citation Information

The following chapters were originally published in the *New Review of Children's Literature and Librarianship*, volume 17, issue 2 (November 2011). When citing this material, please use the original page numbering for each article, as follows:

Acknowledgements

The Publisher would like to thank George Brazillar, Trina Schart Hyman, Holiday House, Martin Ripkens and Hans Stempel, Heinz Edelmann, Friedrich Middelhauve Verlag, Thé Tjong-Khing, Jackie Morris, Robert Ingpen, Ann and Paul Rand, Barbara McClintock, Martin Baltscheit and Christine Schwarz, Elisabeth Brami and Claude Cachin, Steven Guarnaccia, Russell Hoban and Garth Williams, the *Sunday Post*, D. C. Thomson & Co, Colin Thompson, Shaun Tan, and Scholastic for their kind permission to reproduce the images included in this book.

Whilst every effort has been made to trace copyright holders, this has not been possible in all cases. Any omissions brought to our attention will be remedied in future editions.

INTRODUCTION

EVELYN ARIZPE, MAUREEN A. FARRELL, and JULIE MCADAM

School of Education and Visual Journeys Research Term, University of Glasgow, Scotland

When we wrote the editorial for this collection of articles, initially published in a special issue of the journal *New Review of Children's Literature and Librarianship* in 2011, Julia Donaldson had just taken over as Children's Laureate from Anthony Browne, the award-winning illustrator who devoted much of his time in this role to raising the profile of picturebooks and promoting visual literacy. We were certain that the focus on both words and pictures would continue during Donaldson's period as Children's Laureate given that, together with illustrator Axel Scheffler, she has created several award-winning picturebooks including that instant classic: *The Gruffalo*. Now, as we write this Introduction, we have seen the extent of Donaldson's commitment to supporting public libraries, an essential task in these difficult financial times in the United Kingdom because one of the things libraries can do is bring together children and the best picturebooks—and, by this, we mean picturebooks that challenge readers, that take readers beyond literal meanings, out of their "comfort zone" and into complex thinking about relationships, the environment, war, reality, and even death. As we all know, in this age where marketing rules, there are many bland and boring illustrated books for children and there are still some parents, teachers, librarians, and educationalists who consider a picturebook to be any simple text with pictures for a very young, pre-literate audience and regard any complex or controversial aspects with suspicion. Fortunately, there are also many who now recognize the picturebook as a sophisticated art form that has provided a space for some of the most exciting innovations in the field of children's literature (sometimes even going beyond innovations in adult literature).

This book brings together nine chapters by a group of expert international scholars, based in the United States, Europe, and the United Kingdom, who present original theoretical perspectives and new research on picturebooks and their readers. The chapters not only provide evidence of the ways in which the best authors and illustrators stretch artistic, narrative, and cultural expectations beyond the traditional stereotype of a picturebook but also how academics and researchers draw on disciplines such as art and cultural history, semiotics, philosophy, cultural geography, literary theory, and visual literacy to do so. The authors revisit the question of what a picturebook is as an object using cultural, artistic, literary and educational perspectives. Some of them look at the socio-historical conditions in which picturebooks have been created in different countries. Some of them point out the variations between picturebooks from different cultures and languages but also highlight the commonalities between them, for example in the appearance of often overlooked but greatly significant objects. The references to international picturebooks are a reminder of the wealth of excellent publications outside the United Kingdom that we should be more aware of. Finally, the authors consider what the stretching of borders may mean for new generations of readers and what contemporary children themselves have to say about them.

In the opening chapter, Barbara Kiefer returns to the origins of art and bookmaking to show how historical changes in technology, culture, and society have influenced the picturebook as an art object and developed it into a dynamic genre. She highlights the commonalities in inspiration and intent between artists and illustrators across the centuries, as they create beautiful illustrations that sometimes literally breach the visual borders and often challenge a confined view of childhood.

It is true that this challenge also raises questions about whether some books are really for children or whether they are just another medium for conducting artistic experiments or communicating particular ideologies. Bettina Kümmerling-Meibauer and Jörg Meibauer tackle this issue in Chapter 2 through the development of the concept of "strangeness" through an analysis of German Pop Art picturebooks from the middle of the twentieth century, some of which even by contemporary standards go beyond the borders of narrative expectations and sense. They argue that the view of childhood as a time of openness to new experiences led Pop Art artists to invite readers to transgress the boundaries of conventions and knowledge of the function and meaning of pictures and text. It led to some interesting experiments such as one in 1970 where a picturebook (with a preface by Jean Piaget) was created based on children's responses to another picturebook. The authors also suggest these books are the precursors of what we now consider "postmodern" picturebooks.

Confined views of what constitutes a picturebook story are also challenged by illustrators through the "paratext," that is, any features that go beyond the actual text but actively enhance it in some way. In Chapter 3, Teresa Duran and Emma Bosch examine the role of endpapers in an extensive corpus of picturebooks in several languages, making us think anew about this often overlooked feature. They describe how endpapers can offer clues, humor, irony, surprises, and sometimes even a "bonus track" for attentive readers.

Chapters 4 and 5 continue with an exploration of visual signifiers that take readers into spaces where narrative interacts with notions of childhood and cultural practices. Maria Nikolajeva and Liz Taylor's in-depth analysis of beds in picturebooks includes both the portrayal and function of this everyday (or rather, everynight) material object along with bedrooms, bedding, and bedtime. The bedtime space which, as the authors argue, is a "highly ambivalent topos," straddles the border between the public and the private as well as between reality and fantasy. The surprising breadth of their examples, drawn from a wide range of international picturebooks, reveals this space as a fundamental site of power negotiations between children and adults.

Cultural signifiers, power, and the position of the child subject are also the considered in Jean Webb's chapter as she takes us through her reading of a "strange" or, more exactly, a "surreal" picturebook in its English version, *When We Lived in Uncle's Hat* by Peter Stamm and Jutta Bauer. But, these signifiers go beyond the picturebook itself, extending into the transformations undergone by the words and pictures during translation and for publicity as well as into the reading offered by the notes for teachers. Webb challenges the simplistic reading suggested by these notes by highlighting the more subtle connections required from the reader for understanding the different atmospheres and emotions that deal with displacement, dislocation, and family relationships. Yet these are not "real" locations; as Webb argues, the "text moves beyond the boundaries of 'normal' existence" into the realm of the imagination, demanding a different reading. She shows how the philosophical lenses of both surrealism and existentialism are helpful in meeting this demand.

Cultural borders are the main focus of Maureen A. Farrell's whirlwind tour of Scottish texts and images in Chapter 6 as she raises questions about what it means to stay within or go beyond the borders of a particular culture. Text and image in multicultural picturebooks are often a source of debate: How far should inherited boundaries be respected and preserved? Should new cultural combinations and cosmopolitanism be encouraged? Who is entitled to portray a particular cultural context? Seeking answers to these questions, Farrell discusses a range of images from well-loved comics to ancient ballads to contemporary picturebooks. She shows how traditional stereotypes are being subverted and new cosmopolitan identities that are rooted in the local but that look to the global provide the opportunity for a more distinct national identity and at the same time a more inclusive one.

The final three chapters consider the crossing of borders from the perspective of the readers. They look at the responses of readers from different countries and backgrounds highlighting the potential of picturebooks for exploring (among other things) art, illustration, and design; the relationship between text and image; and other places and cultures. In Chapter 7, Janet Evans returns to the question previously raised about complex and controversial subject matter as she discusses children's responses to another "strange" picturebook that shares some of the existential questions of *When We Lived in Uncle's Hat* in terms of happiness, relationships, and the possession of material objects. The children in Evans' study reflect and talk about the "purpose of life" based on Colin Thompson and Amy Lissiat's book, *The Short and Incredibly Happy Life of Riley* (2005). Evans presents evidence that participating in collaborative discussion about a picturebook that invites children to go beyond the words and the images through the peritext, the intertextual references, and the links to current world events can be a powerful way of increasing readers' understanding and engagement with ideas.

A similar situation is presented in the next two chapters which present findings related to the two wordless picturebooks read by children within the context of a research project, *Visual Journeys*.[1] Their wordless nature take readers beyond the borders of written language and challenge readers to find other ways of "filling the gaps." In Chapter 8, Brenda Bellorín and María Cecilia Silva-Díaz look at the analysis of a group discussion around *The Arrival* by Shaun Tan to see how young readers fill the indeterminacies created by visual language which are particularly related to the mental processes of the characters. Without the words to help, readers are forced to rely on visual clues and their own experiences to interpret thoughts and emotions. The other wordless book used in the project, *Flotsam* by David Wiesner, also demanded close review. In the final chapter, Evelyn Arizpe and Julie McAdam describe how responding to this book through a photographic activity allowed insights into the meaning-making processes of readers. Given that the theme of the picturebook is the power and mystery of photographs and that Wiesner plays with many of the techniques of photography to tell its story, this activity turned out to be a way for a group of diverse readers, which included immigrant children, to control representations of their identity and, at the same time, increase awareness of the construction and metalanguage of image.

The implication that emerges from this collection of scholarly research is that space for children to look and talk about picturebooks is an essential part of reading—both in and out of school and with both peers and adults. As twenty-first century children become more used to fast-moving images on screens, they need to be reminded to stop and look closely, to discover the pleasure of finding clues and making meaning with them, particularly when they are challenged to go beyond their usual expectations. Complex picturebooks do stir up all sorts of emotions, fear, sadness, joy, but we must trust the child reader to handle this experience—or to reject it or ask or show signs of needing help if they cannot. What picturebooks offer is just too important to be left to grownups' responses, however well-intentioned they may be. Children can also be encouraged to extend picturebook reading through other creative activities, for example, as editors who work with educational settings, we could image an exercise in visual literacy that encouraged young readers to find books with interesting endpapers, to classify them using the typology similar to that described by Duran and Bosch and to draw their own endpapers for particular books.

Included in this space and in the process of discovery should be picturebooks that go beyond one's own culture and language. It is perhaps understandable that British audiences fail to look beyond publications in English, given the wealth of picturebooks that exist in this language, but this produces an insular and narrow perspective that misses out on the fascinating developments in Europe and in other countries. Thanks to a few determined publishers such as Winged Chariot, translations of some recent European picturebooks, such as the aforementioned one examined by Jean Webb, are now available in English. However, many of those mentioned by other contributors would also be well worth translating. We thus take advantage of this Introduction to call to teachers, librarians, publishers, and others involved in promoting and marketing books to go beyond national and cultural frontiers.

Most of these chapters were originally presented as papers in the second conference on Picturebook Research held at the University of Glasgow in 2009 "Beyond Borders: Art, narrative and culture in picturebooks." The aim of this ongoing series of conferences is to provide a space for ideas and discussion on new theoretical perspectives and cutting-edge research into the burgeoning picturebook market and their readers. This collection builds on previous publications resulting from this conference series: *New Impulses in Picturebook Research* edited by Kümmerling-Meibauer, Colomer, and Silva-Díaz, published in English (Routledge) and also in Spanish (Banco del Libro/GRETEL) and the forthcoming *Aesthetic and Cognitive Challenges of the Picturebook* (Routledge) also edited by Kümmerling-Meibauer. As the editors, we would like to thank all the contributors to the present volume for their insightful contributions and we are grateful for their hard work and patience. We were delighted that Sally Maynard accepted our proposal for the original special issue and thank her for all her encouragement. We are also grateful to Emily Ross, our Routledge editor, for her support during the process of its publication in book form.

We hope that this collection will be successful in continuing to provide new vistas for picturebook studies, vistas which go beyond all kinds of borders.[2] We want to be able to look to a future where the borders are flexible and permeable, where the potential of picturebooks can reach a diversity of readers through different mediums, literary, and pedagogic approaches: a future that includes the recovery of lesser known, experimental perhaps, picturebooks that can encourage creativity and international exchange not only among young children but also among adolescents and adults.

Notes

1 The aim of this on-going project is to explore how the children construct meaning from visual images in complex narratives in order to create strategies that will develop their critical literacy skills, as well as help them reflect on their own or others' experiences of migration, journeys, and foreign worlds. The international partners involved in the project are the University of Glasgow; the Universitat Autònoma de Barcelona; Teachers College, Columbia University; the Australian Catholic University, NSW, and the University of Bologna. Visual Journeys was funded in the UK

by grants from the Faculty of Education, University of Glasgow, and the United Kingdom Literacy Association (UKLA) (see Arizpe, Colomer and Martínez-Roldán, *Visual Journeys through Wordless Picturebooks: An International Inquiry with Immigrant Children*, forthcoming 2013, Bloomsbury Academic). The work continues to be developed in Glasgow through a grant from The Esmée Fairbairn Foundation.

2 As an indication of the growing interest in picturebook research, a JISCMail group called *New Directions in Picturebook Research*, was set up to continue scholarly exchange on this topic. It gained 140 subscribers from all over the world in the first two weeks of opening. https://www.jiscmail.ac.uk/cgi-bin/webadmin?A0=PICTUREBOOKRESEARCH

WHAT IS A PICTUREBOOK? ACROSS THE BORDERS OF HISTORY

BARBARA KIEFER

The Ohio State University, Columbus, Ohio, USA

In this article I contemplate the ideas of art, narrative, and culture in picturebooks from a historical perspective. In particular, I define a picturebook as a visual verbal entity and explore the question, "How has the form of the picturebook manifested itself throughout human history?" I look at how changes in technology, culture, and society have influenced the picturebook as an art object from prehistoric times to the present day. Finally, I examine the role of the picturebook artist across the centuries and find common similarities in inspiration, intent, and motivation that link these artists despite the differences in the form and audience for picturebooks over time.

Wondering about children's preference for style in picturebooks, I asked a seven-year-old if Chris Van Allsburg's black and white illustrations in *Jumanji* would have been better in color. ""Pictures don't have to be in color . . . It's harder when it's in black and white. It takes more time and you don't just whip through the book. . . . You like to take time," he replied." What more could one hope for in children's responses to picturebooks: to take <u>time</u> with a book.

Questions regarding children and picturebooks have been the focus of much of my research as I studied children ages 6 through 11 in school classrooms (Kiefer). I began my research with a rather superficial question—"What type of illustrations do children <u>like</u> in picturebooks." I have since realized that a better question is "How do they respond to a variety of picturebooks in a variety of styles and formats?" This allowed me to focus more broadly on the wide range of cognitive and emotional reactions that children may have and on the ways in which responses change over time.

Indeed, I found that the children ages 6–11 that I studied were intent on making meaning of the art that they were seeing. Often these children helped me to look at picturebooks more carefully and to see things that I had never understood in the illustrations, despite my Bachelor of Arts in Art education.

Moreover, I found that in order to better understand the responses of modern day children I had to better understand aesthetic response to art in a broader sense myself, asking in more depth, "What is a picturebook?" and "How has the art form of the picturebook manifested itself throughout human history?"

Scholarly investigations of the picturebook over the last four decades have helped to define not only what a picturebook is as a cultural object but also how it works to engender aesthetic experiences in the reader. One widely quoted definition comes from Barbara Bader's study of American children's picturebooks in the twentieth century. Bader wrote:

> A picturebook is text, illustrations, total design; an item of manufacture and a commercial product; a social, cultural, historical document; and foremost an experience for a child. As an art form it hinges on the interdependence of pictures and words, on the simultaneous display of two facing pages, and on the drama of the turning page. (1)

Bader's definition drew our attention to the child audience for the picturebook, and the social, cultural, and technological factors that influenced the form and audience for picturebooks of the twentieth century. She also emphasized the unique qualities of the picturebook as an art object and the words and images that worked together to engender response as pages were turned. At a time when most reviews of picturebooks gave heed to the text with (perhaps) a sentence mentioning the illustrations, art educator Kenneth Marantz insisted that "picturebooks are not literature, that is, word dominated things, but rather a form of visual art. The picturebook must be experienced as a visual/verbal entity if its potential values are to be realized." (1983, 151)

Other researchers soon took those definitions further, developing theories of how pictures and texts work to create meaning.

Nodelman explored the semiotic function of details in the illustrations in picturebooks and how they contribute to a book's meaning. Nicolajeva and Scott built on the work of Nodelman and others to provide an in-depth exploration of how the "'text' was created by the interaction of verbal and visual information" for decoding a specific picturebook (5).

All these researchers have provided us with ever deepening understandings of today's picturebooks. However, for many years illustrators have been treated as craftsman rather than fine artists and the picturebook has been looked down on as childish. Instead, my research with children and my studies in art history, particularly medieval art, led to a desire to trace the roots of today's picturebooks across the borders of history.

Espousing the argument that the picturebook is a visual/verbal entity, I believe it is possible to trace the art object to prehistoric forms. Over thirty thousand years ago the cave painters of Lascaux and Chauve-Pont-d'Arc used the technology at hand—charcoal, minerals or plant-based pigments, brush tools and stone walls— to create these exquisite images. We do not know, of course, the context in which the paintings were viewed, but it is not hard to imagine that there were ceremonies of some sort, that is, words or chants that were viewed by an awed audience of people of the time. Perhaps it is not too farfetched to find the same rapt attention of some prehistoric audience in a contemporary classroom of children held enthralled as their teacher shares a picturebook.

If this seems too fanciful, then surely we can progress to ancient Egypt to find the combination of visual and verbal that Marantz describes. Editions of the *Book of the Dead*, meant to provide guidance to souls on their journeys to the afterlife, were beautifully designed visual/verbal entities, drawings on papyrus scrolls that were read in linear fashion.

Around the first century, the Romans developed the codex, a technological innovation that changed the picturebook into the form we still have today. This technique allowed bookmakers to cut pieces of papyrus or parchment into sheets, which were folded and sewn together in the fold, then bound with thin pieces of wood covered with leather. Moreover, the codex changed layout and design in books. Full-page, framed illustrations— sometimes alone, sometimes facing a page of printed text—were the result of this form. The invention of the codex, according to Jonathon Harthan, "affected book production as profoundly and permanently as did the invention of printing in the mid-fifteenth century" (12).

The codex form allowed a wider range of style and media to be used in the illustrations. Since layers of paint would crack when rolled and unrolled, rolled scrolls were executed mostly with line drawings. In addition, papyrus rapidly disintegrated in the Mediterranean climate beyond Egypt. As the new codex form moved north and west papyrus was replaced by parchment or vellum, made of animal skins. The codex form and the parchment page made possible the use of rich colors, including gold for illustrations.

Some of the picturebooks of the Middle Ages included secular topics. Bestiaries were popular types as were illustrations of romances such as the tales of King Arthur. However, the church was largely responsible for the development of medieval illuminated manuscripts. These religious books took many forms—Gospels, Psalters and Graduals or hymn books, and Apocalypses. The styles of the earliest manuscripts developed from two major styles, the Byzantine, which relied on Greco-Roman style, and the Insular which reflected styles and motifs of Celtic art that survived in the British Isles. The illustrations in the Insular manuscripts were predominately ornamental and included interlacing, beast ribbon designs, and spiral patterns such as those found in the *Book of Kells* (800 CE) or the *Lindisfarne Gospels* (690 CE). Gradually, these two artistic styles began to intermingle and change. By the tenth century, Western illustration was becoming more individualized and dynamic as well as more elaborate.

It was common in the Middle Ages to place the Old and New Testaments into separate sections. Thus, the types of manuscripts that developed for use in religious services included Gospels, Psalters, Lectionaries, and Graduals. Specific iconography and patterns of composition were found in each of these different forms. Beginning in the thirteenth century, several forms were developed that are visually similar to today's picturebooks in their page design and balance of image and word. These include the Bible Moralize, Bible Pauperum, and Bible Histoire. These often had short biblical passages and commentaries with allegorical lessons and emphasized the connections between the Old and New Testaments. The British Library owns the *Kings 5*, a Bible Pauperum that is remarkably similar to a picturebook of today. Rather than the typical vertical orientation of medieval manuscripts that resulted from the folded gatherings of parchment, the Kings 5 is horizontal, the result of gluing three pieces of parchment together. Only the right hand half of each double page spread is illustrated as if to draw viewer's attention on a single message. The central section holds the largest painting, a depiction of a major scene from the life of Christ. Taking up about two thirds of the central section, the picture is framed by a rectangular decorated border. Flowing banners on three sides carry important ideas pertaining to the picture, accompanied by smaller faces of important saints. Underneath the paintings a paragraph of explication is printed in three different colors. The left and right sections of the page also contain brief colored paragraphs of text and bordered biblical scenes. These depict stories from the Old Testament that presage the New Testament event.

By the twelfth century, the content of illuminated manuscripts, while still sacred, expanded into books popular with lay populations. Books of hours began to be used for private devotions of the wealthy. Along with biblical passages and devotions, these books always included calendars to mark important religious days throughout the year. It became a tradition to divide the Calendar into the twelve months of the year and to illustrate each month with a scene of secular life.

A New Technology

Several major technological advances took place during the Middle Ages that affected book availability and production. The first was the development of paper, which may have spread to Europe from China through Islamic countries. This material was not as strong as parchment but it was much cheaper and by the thirteenth century methods of paper production were being perfected by such firms as Fabriano in Italy. At about the same time, inks the proper consistency for woodblock printing were developed as did a method of printing, in which letters and pictures were cut into a single block. The great revolution in book production, however, came with the invention of the printing press with movable type during the 1450s. This invention signaled the end of the hand-illuminated book and the beginning of picturebook making as a commercial rather than a purely aesthetic process.

The illuminated manuscript did not, of course, disappear overnight; it coexisted for many years with typeset forms. Other mechanically printed books were illustrated by hand even though the woodblock was widely known and ideally suited to the type-set text. At other times, the wood block was used for illustrations, but only to produce the simplest of outlines, which were then colored in by hand. Eventually the standards of beauty set by the illuminated manuscripts were set aside for the expediency of print making. Instead, the artists of the page took their interest in genre scenes and decorated borders to painting on a single canvas in oil. The picturebook survived but would need several centuries to mature as a new art form for children.

In 1744, influenced by John Locke and ideas of the Age of Enlightenment, John Newbery published *A Little Pretty Pocket-Book* considered the first book created for the entertainment of children. Newbery's commercial success inspired other publishing firms to create books for children. By the beginning of the 1800's, children's picturebooks—the true integration of the verbal and visual for the entertainment of a young audience—were becoming popular. William Roscoe's fanciful *The Butterfly's Ball and the Grasshopper's Feast* with hand-colored illustrations inspired a host of similar titles.

During the nineteenth century, printing techniques improved and illustrated newspapers and magazines became popular. Magazines such as the satirical *Punch*, first published in 1841, attracted talented artists such as Edward Lear, John Tenniel, Richard Doyle, and Hablot "Phiz" Brown. Tenniel, Doyle, Brown and others were soon commissioned to provide illustrations for children's books and brought their wry senses of humor to picturebook illustrations. Charles H. Bennett, one of these artists, created some remarkably lively picturebooks. His *Nine Lives of a Cat* published in 1860 has the brevity of text, the witty illustrations, and the attention to page layout and design that is typical of the best twentieth century children's picturebooks.

For much of the nineteenth century the search for effective and inexpensive color reproduction was paramount. Aside from studio experiments like the colored etchings of William Blake, color had to be added to prints by hand, using brush or stencil. The credit for achieving color reproduction for a large market must go to publisher Edmund Evans. By the 1860s, Evans, an artist himself, made a real effort to refine the process of color printing. Brian Alderson suggests:

> There is no gainsaying the care which Edmund Evans gave to the early print-runs of his picturebooks, if not always the later ones. The "clever artist" in him recognized the need for printing techniques to match the illustrator's work as closely as possible and he was one of the pioneers in applying photographic processes to the preparation of woodblocks. He was also sensitive to colour-values and how they could be mingled through the overprinting of tints, and he exercised great care in his choice of pigments for his inks. (75)

With this attention to detail, Evans enlisted accomplished artists like Walter Crane and Kate Greenaway to create works especially for children. In their books, often collections of nursery rhymes or songs, we see a real interaction between pictures and words in addition to pleasing color reproduction and total book design. In 1878 Randolph Caldecott worked with Evans to create *The Diverting History of John Gilpin* one of the first of his many popular books for children.

Thanks to Evans's techniques in England, the field of illustration for children would go on to attract now-legendary figures that included Beatrix Potter, Arthur Rackham, Leslie Brooke, and Ernest Shepard, while America would give us Howard Pyle, N.C. Wyeth, and Jessie Wilcox Smith. In 1927, *Clever Bill* was written and illustrated by English artist William Nicholson and was followed in 1928 by American illustrator Wanda Gag's *Millions of Cats*. These stories were told with very little text and relied heavily on the illustrations to convey meaning, a format that predominates in children's picturebooks through much of the twentieth century. Their publication marked a new era of picturebook publishing.

The Artist: Connections Across the Borders of Time

The picturebook as an art object has undergone many changes over the centuries as a result of societal, technological, and other influence. What I find remarkable is that the personality or intent of the artist during these years has remained so similar.

Artists are Observers and Chroniclers of Their Worlds

For many centuries picturebook artists have provided us with first hand observations of human society that serve as historic records as well as aesthetic objects (see Figures 1 and 2). In the calendar, pages of the books of hours such as *Tres Riche Heures du Duc de Berry*, we see the lives of the privileged and the peasantry as they were lived in the early fifteenth century. At the end of the twentieth century, in *A Child's Calendar*, Trina Schart Hyman took us through the months of the year to illustrate poems by John Updike. In Hyman's view, instead of royals and peasants, we see a middle class multiracial family at work and play in over a twelve month period.

In 1440 the artist of the *Hours of Catherine of Cleves* depicted a cozy home interior. Titled "The Holy Family at Work," the image shows the family in the kitchen, Joseph planing a block of wood, Mary weaving at a loom, and Baby Jesus in a fifteen century walker. Compare this to Maurie J. Manning's *Kitchen Dance*, published in 2008. This book also depicts a warm family scene, with two Latino youngsters peeking through a door to watch their mother and father dance as they clean up the kitchen.

Just as book artists have found everyday life appealing subjects, artists have been intrigued by the same texts and characters over the years. Aesop's Fables have long been of interest to illustrators. We can find Aesop in a tenth century manuscript, a version printed in 1485, one engraved by Francis Barlow in 1666 and Jerry Pinkney's version of Aesop's *The Lion and the Mouse*, published in 2009.

Animals have also held tremendous appeal to illustrators and have found their ways into the pages of books. Tales of dragons and heroes have been particularly popular with artists. We can find "Dragons Saint George Slaying the Dragon" in a Belgian manuscript created around 1430 or a Persian *Shah-nama* "Bahram Gur Killing the Dragon" painted in 1511. In 1985 Trina Schart Hyman won a Caldecott award for *Saint George and the Dragon* retold by Margaret Hodges.

Domestic animals, particularly cats and dogs, have appeared consistently in illustrated texts. The monk who scripted the Reichenau Primer, which dates from the 8th century, included a poem to his cat, Pangur Ban. Cats often feature in Trina Schart

FIGURE 1 Slip Cover. *The Tres Riche Heures of Jean, Duke of Berry* from publisher George Brazillar (color figure available online).

FIGURE 2 Illustration copyright (c) 1999 by Trina Schart Hyman. Reprinted from *A Child's Calendar* by John Updike by permission of Holiday House (color figure available online).

Hyman's books such as *Little Red Riding Hood*, published in 1983. Cats still feature prominently in children's books today, depicted in styles as various as Linda Newbery and Catherine Rayner's *Posy* and Lark Pien's *Long Tail Kitty*.

In the Middle Ages dogs often appeared as a symbol of spiritual faithfulness. Modern day illustrators show a similar faithfulness to dogs. Maurice Sendak's beloved German Shepard is depicted in his *Outside Over There*, published in 1981. Chris Van

Allsburg is even more loyal to an imaginary dog who appears in his first picturebook, *The Garden of Abdul Gasazi,* (published in 1979) and who can be found in some form in all of his subsequent picturebooks.

Artists are Postmodernists No Matter What the Era

Much has been written recently about the trends in postmodern picturebooks in the twenty-first century (Lewis; Panteleo; Sipe and Panteleo). Lewis argues that postmodernism is "the cultural and intellectual phenomena that have grown out of the rubble" of the certainties of Enlightenment to the uncertainties and doubts about present day realities (88). Characteristics of postmodernism include metafictive devices meant to disrupt our expectations of traditional structures of images or textual forms. I would like to borrow some of these postmodern categories or descriptors and add a few themes of my own to argue that post-modernism is not a new phenomenon but a continuation of what book artists have been doing for centuries. In addition to being observer and chroniclers, book illustrators are self-referential, playful and ironic, and intertextual. Finally, they push conventions of design and visual depicting through the art form that is a picturebook.

Artists are Self-Referential

Illustrators seem to love including images of themselves in the pages of their books. In the illuminated manuscripts this may have been their only chance for self-expression as their identities were not recorded in earlier years of illuminated manuscripts. In a Moralized Bible, created in France (*ca.* 1235), we see the author of the work dictating the book to his scribe. A page in the *Stockholm Saint Jerome* shows the scribe, and the illuminator and his helper in the lower margin. In the late twelfth century, Frater Rufillus of Weissenau depicts himself painting a *Passionale.*

More recently Chris Van Allsburg inserted a self-portrait in *The Wreck of the Zephyr* published in 1991. Trina Schart Hyman and her family members often appear in her books. Trina herself is the main character in Margaret Kimmel's *Magic in the Mist* (1984) and she can be found as a medieval illuminator on the back cover of Hodges's *Saint George and the Dragon*.

Artists are Playful

Artists have exhibited humor and playfulness for centuries. At the same time that versions of the sacred *Book of the Dead* were being created (*ca.* 1295–1069 BCE), an artist illustrated a comical "Papyrus with Satirical Vignettes" showing a group of animals walking upright in a parade and a lion and an antelope, natural enemies, grinning at each other over a board game.

This sense of humor often led to ironic depictions or parodies. Many of the sacred texts of the Middle Ages contained comical beast and earthy images in their margins (see Michael Camille's *Image on the Edge: The Margins of Medieval Art*). *The Morgan Library Manuscript 358*, a book of hours created around 1445, has a marginal painting showing a rabbit doctor holding a urine sample as two dogs on crutches approach for treatment.

Some of these border paintings could be considered quite rude, showing very profane images alongside the sacred. A book of hours belonging to the Bodleian Library, shows a border painting titled "Young man led to the 'Gates of Hell,'" and depicts a man viewing a couple engaged in intercourse. In the twentieth century, Trina Schart Hyman drew criticism from some conservatives for her illustrations for Howard Pyle's *King Stork* (1973). In one double page spread she shows an evil witch sitting at a carved wooden table. On one side of the table's edge a skull is carved; on the other edge, a naked couple is shown in a carnal embrace. Hyman also raised alarm by inscribing a tombstone in *Will You Sign Here, John Hancock?* (by Jean Fritz, 1976) with the words "Virginia Kirkus, a nasty soul is its own reward." This reference to a well-known children's book review journal that had been less than kind in reviews of some of her work alarmed her publisher enough to remove it from subsequent editions.

Artists are Intertextual

Much has been made of the phenomenon of intertextuality or pastiche in literature and popular culture. The blending or borrowing from visual texts is quite common in the history of the picturebook. Illuminators often consulted other manuscripts for their pictorial content and page design. Another form of inter-textuality can be found in books of hours or picture Bibles where illuminators depict Old Testament scenes that presage events in the New Testament. In the British Library's *Kings 5*, sidebars depict Gideon and Jacob wrestling with angels, while in the main image a doubting Thomas approaches a wounded Christ.

Modern illustrators have found inspiration from and make reference to paintings and painters from art history. Pieter Brueghel's "Hunters in the Snow" is referenced in one of Errol le Cain's images in *The Snow Queen* by Hans Christian Andersen. Brueghel's "Landscape with the Fall of Icarus" also seems to have inspired one of Maurice Sendak's double page spreads in *Outside Over There*. In the same book Sendak also pays homage to "The Hülsenbeck Children" by nineteenth century German romantic painter Philip Otto Runge.

Chris Van Allsburg has also been influenced by the work of a variety of painters, from twentieth century landscapes of American Grant Wood in *The Stranger*, to the moody landscapes of German Romantic Casper David Frederick in *The Wreck of the Zephyr* and *The Polar Express*. The perspectives and spatial qualities of eighteenth century architect and engraver Giovanni Piranesi (1720–1778) are featured in Van Allsburg's *Garden of Abdul Gasazi* as well as David Wiesner's *Free Fall*.

Finally, we can find the quality of intertextuality in the ongoing work of illustrators such as David Wiesner and David Macaulay. The ripped pages, the pigs, and the dragon that appear in the Caldecott winning *The Three Pigs* (2001), first show up in his *Free Fall* published in 1988. David Macaulay's rampaging cows the cut across stories in his Caldecott Award winning *Black and White* (1990) make their first attempts at mischief in *Why the Chicken Crossed the Road*, published in 1987.

Artists Push Boundaries

A notable characteristic of the best book artists is their tendency to push the boundaries and borders of visual depiction. The papyruses of ancient Egypt are notable examples of visual design as were the printed picturebooks of the seventeenth century. In the nineteenth century artists also gave consideration to total book and page design. The use of the strip or panel layout can be traced back through the Egyptian papyruses (see Scott McCloud's *Understanding Comics*, 1993) through to Raymond Brigg's books to the Shaun Tan's compelling, *The Arrival* (2008).

Importantly, the book artist has been responsible for breaking through conventional depictions of an era to move the history of art into new avenues of thinking about visual art. As calendar page scenes and decorative borders of medieval manuscripts influenced the genre painters and still life painters of the seventeenth century, book artists have moved picturebooks in new directions. For many years paintings in Books of Hours were highly decorative, lovely works of art. For example, the miniatures in the Limbourg Brothers' *Tres Riche Heures du Duc de Berry*, were elegant, balanced and frozen in space, with all images carefully contained within a painted border. Working at the same time as the Limbourg Brothers, however, was an unnamed painter known as the Rohan Master. In his *Book of Hours* he begins to push images outside contained borders. A double page spread shows Noah in a miniature on the left and Saint Mark in a larger miniature on the right. The painter extends the foot of a sleeping Noah out of the border and into the test and he raises a single flag from the castle in the background above Saint Mark above the border of the painting. Even more notable is the emotional quality of the paintings throughout the book. These are not figures posed and frozen in time but real, suffering human beings in all the ugliness of their agony.

Surely we could compare this breakthrough with the work of illustrators such as John Steptoe and Charles Keeping in the twentieth century who broke away from the idealized childhoods of Marie Hall Ets or Lois Lenski to depict children in their cultural and emotional fullness.

Conclusion

Through the centuries, the artist's role has been to understand the needs of society and, using the technology at hand, to convey some meaning through the pages of a picturebook. Throughout the years the creators of picturebooks have been people who had some inner need to tell about their world through pictures, to respond to societal needs but also to push the boundaries of visual depiction. Play, a sense of irony, subversion of convention and other aspects of the post-modern picturebook can be found in many eras. What seems clear is that picturebooks will continue to evolve and change but that the powerful partnership of image and idea will continue to delight human audiences of all ages and to attract artists to explore the human condition.

References

Alderson, Brian. *Sing a Song for Sixpence: The English Picture Book Tradition and Randolph Caldecott*. Cambridge England: Cambridge University Press, 1986. Print.

Bader, Barbara. *American Picture Book from Noah's Ark to The Beast Within*. New York: Macmillan, 1976. Print.

Barlow, Francis. *Aesop's Fables*. London: H. Hills, 1687. Print.

The Book of Kells. Trinity College: Dublin, Ireland, ca. 800.

Briggs, Raymond. *Father Christmas*. London, UK: Penguin, 1973. Print.

Caldecott, Randolph. *The Diverting History of John Gilpin*. London: Routledge, 1878. Print.

Camille, Michael. *Image on the Edge: The Margins of Medieval Art*. Cambridge MA: Harvard University Press, 1992. Print.

Gag, Wanda. *Millions of Cats*. New York: Coward- McCann, 1928. Print.

Harthan, John. *The History of the Illustrated Book: The Western Tradition*. New York: Thames and Hudson, 1981. Print.

Kiefer, Barbara. *The Potential of Picturebooks: From Visual Literacy to Aesthetic Understanding*. Columbus, OH: Merrill, 1995. Print.

Kings 5 Biblia Pauperum. British Library, ca. 1405.

Limbourg Brothers. *The Très Riche Heures of Jean, Duc de Berry*. Ca.1412–1416.

Lindesfarne Gospels. British Museum, London, 7th–8th century A.D.

Lewis, David. *Reading Contemporary Picturebooks: Picturing Text*. London: Routledge, 2001.

Marantz, Kenneth. "The Picture Book as Art Object: A Call for Balanced Reviewing." *Signposts to Criticism of Children's Literature*. Ed. Robert Bator. Chicago: American Library Association, 1983. 152–55. Print.

The Master of Catherine of Cleves. "The Holy Family At Work" in *Hours of Catherine of Cleves*. Utrecht, ca. 1440.

McCloud, Scott. *Understanding Comics: The Invisible Art*. New York: HarperCollins, 1993. Print.

The Moralized Bible of Blanche de Castile. France, ca. 1235.

Nicholson, William. *Clever Bill*. London: Heinemann, 1926. Print.

Nicolajeva, Maria, and Carole Scott. *How Picturebooks Work*. London: Garland Publishing, 2001. Print

Nodelman, Perry. *Words About Pictures: The Narrative Art of Children's Picture Books*. Athens, GA: University of Georgia Press, 1988. Print

"Pangur Ban." *Reichenau Primer*. Ca 800.

Panteleo, Sylvia. *Exploring Student Response to Contemporary Picturebooks*. Toronto: University of Toronto Press, 2008. Print

Papyrus with Satirical Vignette. Probably from Thebes. British Museum, London, ca. 1295–1069 B.C.

Rohan Master. *The Grand Hours of Rohan*. Paris: Bibliotèque National, ca 1430–1435.

Roscoe, William. *The Butterfly's Ball and the Grasshopper's Feast*. London: J. Harris, 1808. Print.

Rufillus, R. *Passional*. Weisenthal, Germany, ca. 1170–1200.

Sipe, Lawrence R., and Sylvia Panteleo. *Postmodern Picturebooks; Play, Parody and Self-Referentiality*. New York: Routledge, 2008. Print.

Tan, Shaun. *The Arrival*. NY: Scholastic, 2007. Print.

Van Eyck, Barthelemy. *Book of Hours*. France: Aix-en- Province, ca. 1445.

"Young Man Led to the Gates of Hell." *Psalter*. Bodleian Library, ca. 1320–1330.

Children's Literature

Andersen, Hans Christian. *The Snow Queen*. Illus. Erroll LeCain. New York: Puffin, 1982. Print.

Fritz, Jean. *Will You Sign Here, John Hancock?* Illus. Trina Schart Hyman. New York: Coward-McCann, 1976. Print.

Grimm Brothers. *Little Red Riding Hood*. Illus. Trina Schart Hyman. New York: Holiday House, 1983. Print.

Hodges, Margaret. *Saint George and the Dragon*. Illus. Trina Schart Hyman. Boston: Little Brown, 1984. Print.

Kimmel, Margaret. *Magic in the Mist*. Illus. Trina Schart Hyman. New York: Macmillan, 1975. Print.

Macaulay, David. *Black and White*. Boston: Houghton Mifflin, 1990. Print.

—. *Why the Chicken Crossed the Road*. Boston: Houghton Mifflin, 1987. Print.

Manning, Maurie J. *Kitchen Dance*. Boston: Houghton, 2008. Print.

Newbery, Linda. *Posy*. Illus. Catherine Raynor. New York: Atheneum, 2008. Print.

Pien, Lark. *Long Tail Kitty*. Maplewood, NJ: Blue Apple, 2009. Print.

Pinkney, Jerry. *The Lion and the Mouse*. Boston: Little Brown, 2009. Print.

Pyle, Howard. *King Stork*. Illus. Trina Schart Hyman. Boston: Little Brown, 1973 Print.

Sendak, Maurice. *Outside Over There*. New York: Harper & Row, 1981 Print.

Updike, John. *A Child's Calendar*. Illus. Trina Schart Hyman. New York: Holiday House, 1999. Print.

Van Allsburg, Chris. *The Garden of Abdul Gasazi*. Boston: Houghton Mifflin, 1979. Print.

—. *Jumanji*. Boston: Houghton Mifflin, 1981. Print.

—. *The Polar Express*. Boston: Houghton Mifflin, 1985. Print.

—. *The Stranger*. Boston: Houghton Mifflin, 1986. Print.

—. *The Wreck of the Zephyr*. Boston: Houghton Mifflin. 1983. Print.

Wiesner, David. *Free Fall*. New York : Lothrop, Lee & Shepard Books, 1988. Print.

—. *The Three Pigs*. New York: Clarion, 2001. Print.

ON THE STRANGENESS OF POP ART PICTUREBOOKS: PICTURES, TEXTS, PARATEXTS

BETTINA KÜMMERLING-MEIBAUER

German Department, University of Tübingen, Tübingen, Germany

JÖRG MEIBAUER

German Department, University of Mainz, Mainz, Germany

As a species of picturebook emerging around 1970, some Pop Art picturebooks were quite successful in their time, but appear strange from today's point of view. This strangeness has to do with multiple transgressions of traditional conventions restricting the notion of a "good" picturebook: transgressions regarding artistic style (influenced by the Pop Art movement), transgressions regarding the stories' content (with their emphasis on weird characters, surprising twists in narration and plot, and a fanciful combination of sceneries), and transgressions regarding the idea that politics and economic and social problems should be banned from picturebooks (displaying an anti-capitalist or anti-authoritarian attitude). While portraying five Pop Art picturebooks in more detail, the article aims at establishing the notion of strangeness as a descriptive term in picturebook analysis. It is pointed out that strange picturebooks not only erect boundaries for their understanding, but also invite to transgress these boundaries.

Introduction

Pop Art picturebooks are a specific type of picturebooks that emerged around 1970 and was heavily influenced by the art movement called Pop Art. Pop Art is characterized by a permanent transgression of boundaries, for example (1) the shift between fine art and popular art/culture, (2) the contrast between original artwork and reproduction; (3) the revitalization of the European avant-garde, such as Surrealism and Dada, on the one hand, and (4) the indebtedness to the codes and technical processes of mass media on the other hand.

Pop Art mostly deals with material that already exists as a sign, for instance photograph, comic, advertisement, newspaper, and other "pre-coded material" (see Alloway 170). The artists were interested in extending aesthetic attention to the mass media and absorbing mass-media material within the context of art. Further characteristics of Pop Art are the attempt at artistically conveying innovative matters of perception such as, for example, the psychedelic sensual experiences evoked by the consumption of drugs, and the criticism of modern society, politics, and culture.

It appears, then, that Pop Art picturebooks, being overloaded with conflicting messages, run the risk of not being easily understandable for a wider audience, of being strange or weird somehow, of not fitting into the category of "good" picturebooks. What a "good" picturebook is may of course be a matter of taste. However, the assumption that there exist "good" picturebooks— the ones that are recommended by certain social institutions and, for example, distributed by public libraries—is pervasive, not only among parents and teachers, but among scholars, too.

Kiefer (120), for instance, claims that a good picturebook is determined by a stimulating aesthetic experience which derives from the artist's design and technical choices in order to express meaning, and Nodelman points out that: "Many picture books— indeed, possibly all of the best ones—do no just reveal that pictures show us more than words can say; they achieve what Barthes called 'unity on a higher level' by making the difference between words and pictures a significant source of pleasure" (209).

It may be asked, then, whether Pop Art picturebooks are "good" picturebooks in the intended sense.

Note that, when looking at picturebooks, two interests usually interact, the child's interest, maybe the search for pleasure, that has to do with comprehensibility, and the adult's interest that often has to do with (educational) functionality. If a book is too demanding, if it is too radical, it is dysfunctional insofar as that the child is not able to comprehend the multiple levels of meaning necessary for a rough understanding of the respective work.

Comprehensibility, as an important feature for the child's interest in picturebooks, should not be understood as the naïve requirement that everything shown and told in these books has to be cogent from the start; however, the picture-text-relation should be sensitive to the cognitive-developmental stage of the child reader. Although adults and scholars should not underestimate the abilities and curiosity of children, there certainly exist children's books that children cannot easily cope with, simply because of the strangeness of the text and/or pictures. We would like to argue that many Pop Art picturebooks are "strange" indeed and, moreover, that this strangeness appears to be intended.

Although some of the creators of Pop Art picturebooks are famous artists, such as Andy Warhol, Peter Max, Heinz Edelmann (the renowned art director of the Beatles film *The Yellow Submarine*, 1968), and Etienne Delessert, their picturebooks completely fell into oblivion. They are neither mentioned in Barbara Bader's seminal study on American picturebooks nor in any other monographs dedicated to the history and theory of modern picturebooks. (The only references we detected so far are a chapter on picturebooks of the 1960s/1970s in Klaus Doderer's volume on the history of picturebooks in German-speaking countries and an article by Jens Thiele on the influence of pop culture on picturebook artists.)

This obvious neglect in the academia stands in high contrast to the enthusiastic acclaim of Pop Art picturebooks by contemporary critics. Some picturebooks had high print runs, as for instance Eleonore Schmid's and Etienne Delessert's *The Endless Party* (1967), which was translated into 14 languages with more than 4 million copies sold worldwide.

The outline of this article is as follows: First, we focus on five Pop Art picturebooks that show the typical "strange" characteristics of their kind:

- *Story Number 1* (1968). Pictures: Etienne Delessert, Text: Eugène Ionesco
- *The Land of Yellow* (1970). Pictures and Text: Peter Max
- *Rüssel in Komikland* (Nozzle in Comicland 1972). Pictures: Leo Leonhard, Text: Otto Jägersberg
- *Pele sein Bruder* (Pele's Brother 1972). Pictures: Werner Maurer, Text: Jörg Steiner
- *Mister Bird* (1971). Pictures and Text: Parick Couratin

For reasons of space, we will integrate into our analysis aspects of the pictures, the text, and the picture-text-relation; it goes without saying that all of these aspects deserve separate treatment.

Second, we draw attention to some important features of Pop Art picturebooks by stressing the following aspects: title, relationship between illustration and text, and paratexts, such as foreword, afterword, and blurb. The importance of picturebook paratexts was already highlighted by Nikolajeva and Scott (241–62), and we intend to demonstrate that within the realm of Pop Art picturebooks paratexts play significant roles, since they attempt to lead the audience's reception in specific directions.

Finally, we conclude that Pop Art picturebooks transgress certain boundaries of the "good" picturebook, indeed, although clearly these boundaries are in a historical flux and have to be negotiated. Our speculation is that these books were in some ways too demanding and although they obviously reacted to cultural changes, they sometimes overreacted.

Five Pop Art Picturebooks

While the majority of Pop Art picturebooks are so challenging that we suspect that they exceed the child's interpretative abilities, there are some exceptions to the rule. For this reason we will discuss five prototypical Pop Art picturebooks in order to demonstrate, on the one hand, the wide range of artistic styles and genres and, on the other, the different levels of comprehensibility. Moreover, this selection gives an impression of the somewhat complicated texts and complex pictures of Pop Art picturebooks as a whole.

Story Number 1

The best-known Pop Art picturebook is probably *Story Number 1* (1968), with a text by the playwright Eugène Ionesco (from his collection "stories for children under three years of age"), and illustrations by Etienne Delessert. This successful picturebook had three followers: *Story Number 2* (1971), *Story Number 3* (1971), and *Story Number 4* (1973).

Story No 1 is a rather confusing story about a little girl, Josette, who asks her father to tell her a story. In this story, everything, whether people, animals, or toys, has the same name: Jacqueline. Afterwards, when Josette goes shopping with the housekeeper, she meets another girl whose name is Jacqueline and Josette concludes that this girl's parents, siblings, relatives, doll, and even the night potty are named Jacqueline. While the other clients in the shop look worried, the housekeeper keeps calm, since she is accustomed to the silly stories of Josette's father. The text more or less consists of enumerations, even the housekeeper lists the items on the breakfast tray:

> Here is your morning newspaper, here are the postcards you have received, here is your coffee with cream and sugar, here is your fruit juice, here are your rolls, here is your toast, here is your butter, here is your orange marmalade, here is your strawberry jam, here are your fried eggs, here is your ham, and here is your little girl!

The text has no plot at all, apart from the tired father telling his daughter a nonsense story without any plot, and the housekeeper going shopping with the little girl. The protagonists are characterized by a peculiar behavior and communication that is reminiscent of Ionesco's absurd theatre. The oddity of the story is additionally stressed by the watercolor illustrations. Prominent features are the distorted proportions and perspectives, the dreamlike landscapes with strange buildings and fantastic monster-like animals, and the intervisual allusions (for example to the Trojan horse or to Maurice Sendak's picturebook *Where the Wild Things Are* [1963]). Besides the artistic allusions which will mainly be recognized only by adults, this picturebook captivates with the sophisticated use of language. The wordplays and the underlying question of what will happen when everything has the same name, stimulate the viewer's reflection upon the meaning of words and stories. This meaning-making process evokes pleasure and stimulates the child to discover more details in the illustrations that might be overlooked at first glance. While the adult or an older child who is already able to read will obviously detect the signs in the shop that refer to the author, illustrator, publisher, and main figure of the text, children will more easily find pleasure in looking for recurrent motifs, such as the striped clothes, a butterfly, a rhinoceros(!)

reminiscent of Ionesco's most famous theatre play, the little warriors in Antique Greek clothes, or the big eyes. However, the pictures that cover a doublespread without any accompanying text do not directly refer to the story, leaving their interpretation to the viewer, such as the picture presented after Josette's meeting with the girl in the shop: a landscape with mountains and hills is shown against a sunny light background. The biggest mountain has the shape of a human head with curly hair and a face with big eyes from whose holes tiny people are looking out. An endless procession of little folk, all in striped clothes, the women and girls with fair curly hair, the men and boys with a cap on, carrying flags and eye-signs on sticks, is moving across the landscape toward the human-shaped mountain. A monstrous butterfly is sitting on its peak with a throne between his forelegs. The crowned boy on the throne seems to be the goal of the procession, but the connection to the story is not quite clear. Never mind, both story and pictures, even when seen in combination remain strange and indiscernible for adults and children alike. Those who are accustomed to Pop Art and its underlying aesthetic principles, will recognize that Ionesco and Delessert not only refer to nonsense, which has a long tradition within the realm of children's literature, and absurd theatre, which is mainly based on Ionesco's plays, but also to the so-called "aesthetics of boredom" (Alloway 170), regarded by some critics and artists as a main contribution of Pop Art. This aesthetics of boredom is responsible for some eye-catching principles of Pop Art: repetition or serial order, inexpressiveness, obsession with detail of daily life, and abstraction.

The Land of Yellow

Even stranger than *Story Number 1* is *The Land of Yellow* (1970) by Peter Max, famous for his Beatles' posters and disc labels. This book, which is dedicated to the sun, is about colors and tells the story of the purple king who is requested by the sunshine queen to fetch the red color from rainbow land as a tribute to the prince of shadow land. If this request will not be fulfilled, the prince threatens to eliminate all the bright colors by a shadowy grey. The text, written as a poem, describes the journey of the purple king to the different color levels of the rainbow in an enumerative way.

On each page turning, he struggles with another color in order to reach his goal. When he finally catches the red color and fulfills his commitment, he leaves the queen by presenting her a bundle of flowers. The strangeness of this fairytale-like story is additionally stressed by a sylleptic structure: in the lower part of the page a strong dark line divides the illustration into two parts. In this part, faces shown in profile look at each other with speech bubbles coming from their mouths. The short sentences printed in these balloons start with *I am* or *You are*, followed by a noun, such as *poem, sun, poetry,* or *bird*. The connection between these two parts is rather loose; one does not really miss anything from the main story by neglecting this lower part. Yet, the syllepsis contributes to the strangeness of the poem which is characterized by onomatopoetic notions influenced by comics, such as *snap, bam,* and *zip zap*. Even more striking are the illustrations inspired by different Pop Art styles. Peter Max combines collage-like pictures made of marbled paper, cloth, and large spaces painted with acrylic colors. These spaces are either single colored or printed in halftone with a regular dot pattern that reminds the viewer of Roy Lichtenstein's famous paintings. Because of this technique and the merging colors and shapes, it is not always easy to find the figures and faces hidden in the images, most often showing the purple king diving into another color level or running across a fantastic landscape. Peter Max obviously attempts to transfer psychedelic experiences into picturebook art; however, whether children are really attracted by this picture-text-relation remains to be seen. One suspects that the strange depiction of the characters certainly complicates the child's identification with them and their adventures. The anti-narrative structure of *The Land of Yellow* and its heterogeneous visual messages might lead to the assumption that this exceptional work gains status as a rare collectible rather than as a sophisticated book for children.

Rüssel in Komikland

The German picturebook *Rüssel in Komikland* (Nozzle in Comicland 1972) written by Otto Jägersberg and illustrated by Leo Leonhard is characterized by cross-media exchanges and the convergence of multiple layers of meaning, thus adhering to main

principles of the Pop Art movement. The title already refers to
Lewis Carroll's *Alice in Wonderland* (1865), and the first black-and-
white illustrations reminds us of John Tenniel's style. However,
when Nozzle and his friend Bowl start to draw a landscape because
they do not wish to stay in a negative space any longer, the impact
of the fantastic paintings by the Dutch artists Pieter Breughel and
Hieronymus Bosch is prevalent. During their journey through this
strange landscape they meet Flabby Jack, who is painted in full
color and thus contrasts with the unicolored surroundings. Flabby
Jack teaches Nozzle and Bowl how to speak with the help of speech
bubbles, and finally shows them the way to Comicland, where
everything is bright and colorful. The illustrations that depict
the adventures of Nozzle, Bowl and Flabby Jack in Comicland
are framed with a thin black line and structured as panels like
in a comic strip. However, the friends get in trouble by fighting
the mogul Al Bosso who dominates Comicland and its inhabitants with his media empire. In the end they escape Comicland
in search of another country and finally land on a printing press.
By accident they start running the rotation machine that—as the
text explains—prints thousands of copies of the life and adventures of Nozzle and his company in a gigantic process. To stress
the metaphorical meaning of this assertion, the narrator turns
to the readers and tells them that they are actually reading the
story that was printed on this machine. This metafictive ending,
however, is not the only "strange" occurrence in this picturebook
that comprises several metaliterary aspects, such as intertextuality,
intervisuality, metaphors, and irony, as well as a critical perspective
directed against the dominance of the mass media, the individual's powerlessness in an indifferent and egalitarian society, and
the suppression of fantasy and imagination. This picturebook is
obviously overburdened with meaning, artistic allusions, and a
confusing story with an open ending.

Pele sein Bruder

In contrast to *Rüssel in Komikland*, Jörg Steiner's and Werner
Maurer's *Pele sein Bruder* (Pele's Brother 1972) is a picturebook
that draws upon Pop Art for illustrating the impact of perception on worldview. This book tells the story of a little boy who

is scolded for being a "dreamer." Other children laugh at him since he cannot play football, missing the ball every time because of his clumsy movements. The boy withdraws into his own dream world full of fantastic adventures, animals and people. Although he is not completely unhappy, he is worried about the adults' comments on his behavior. The situation changes when he starts school, because the doctor finds out that the boy urgently needs glasses. Due to his short-sightedness he just saw blurred contours and colors, the hazy shadows of moving objects and figures in the surroundings inspired him to invent an own imaginative world. When he wears his glasses, everything becomes clear with straight contours. He can recognize faces and judge distances correctly so that he is then able to participate in the other boys' games, feigning to be the brother of the famous football player Pele. By contrast, when he loans his glasses to other children who have no problems with their eyes, they perceive everything blurred instead, thus getting new insights into the boy's former perception. In this regard, the colorful Pop Art illustrations contribute to successfully convey different visual perspectives on the same object or situation. In this book, the "strangeness" of the pictures is explained by the protagonist's problem with his eye-sight. The picturebook's appeal to tolerance toward disabled people is quite obvious, even though there is no educational instruction in a usual sense.

Mister Bird

As the last example, we consider the picturebook *Mister Bird* (1971) written and illustrated by Patrick Couratin. Mister Bird bears his name because of his hat that he once purchased in exchange for some feathers. In order to satisfy the other birds' longings, he earns his money as a hat seller, until every bird is wearing a hat and called Mister Bird as well. In view of this egalitarian situation, the original Mister Bird does not feel happy anymore. He leaves his companions, searching for a new country where he might regain his individuality.

This poetical fairytale-like text has been completely changed in the German version. The book's title is now *Herr Hut. Nicht Herr Mithut. Nicht Herr Ohnehut. Immer Herr Hut* (Mister Hat. Not Mister

With-hat. Not Mister Without-hat. Always Mister Hat). The first paragraph of the original reads as follows:

> He was called Mister because he wore a hat. And even when—on very rare occasions—he appeared without his hat, all of the other birds would dip their wings politely and say "Good morning, Mister Bird" or "Good evening, Mister Bird." For the others knew that only he had a hat—even if he didn't always wear it. And his hat, after all, was what made him different from the others. Or so it seems.

Now compare the German version:

> Hello. My name is Mister Hat. Quite simply Mister Hat. Sometimes I'm called Musjö Schapo [= Monsieur Chapeau]. This is French and sounds noble. Alas, isn't such a hat noble? And, when the sun shines and it is warm and I leave the hat at home (tree number 18)? Then my name is also Mister Hat. Just as with hat. Not Mister With-hat. Not Mister Without-hat. Always Mister Hat. But everyone knows this, after all. (our translation)

It follows from this short comparison that the German text is far more complicated in that it contains word plays and allusions to foreign languages. The metonymical proper name *Herr Hut* (because the bird always wears a hat) is quite demanding in counter distinction to the English *Mister Bird*. However, during the course of the story, the plot takes another surprising turn. While the original version presents a poetic circumscription of a bird in search of its identity, the German version leads to a critique of capitalist consumerism and egalitarianism which suppress the individuals' needs. As a result, the story ends when Mister Hat intends to emigrate to another country where he might be admired because of his peculiar outlook. But the implied narrator suggests another solution: Mister Hat should throw his hat away or give it to a horse, for example, since flying without a hat is easier. As a conclusion the narrator affirms that "everybody actually knows that," with the implication that only the silly bird Mister Hat has not realized this yet.

In contrast to the majority of Pop Art picturebooks that are distinguished by colorful and bright pictures, Couratin created black-and-white illustrations made with pencil and crayon. The color red constituting a sort of background just appears on the book covers and the endpapers. Therefore, the book conveys a gloomy mood and emphasizes the underlying criticism of the text. The artistic allusion to Pop Art, however, is obvious in the serial order of birds and hats, the rounded shapes of eyes, trees, hills, and faces, and the distorted proportions. The juxtaposition of illustrations and story is another example of boundry transgression.

Titles and Paratexts

Titles

While we find with Pop Art picturebooks the usual types of titles, for example, proper names like Hans Christian Andersen's *Poucette* (Thumbelina 1978) with illustrations by Nicole Claveloux, or Anne van der Essen's *Yok-Yok* (1979), illustrated by Etienne Delessert, or titles rendering the essence of a story, such as *Gertrude and the Mermaid* (1971) by Richard Hughes and Nicole Claveloux, there are stranger, boundary-crossing titles, too. This is in accordance with the provocative, attention-drawing nature of Pop Art picturebooks.

First of all, take the "stories for children under 3 years of age" told by playwright Eugène Ioneco and illustrated by Etienne Delessert as an example. These stories are simply titled *Story No 1* and *Story No 2*. While this pattern reminds the reader of similar practices of enumerating works of art, there is certainly a strong allusion to the prototypicality of these stories. We do not know whether this is to be taken ironically or sincerely, as in many cases of Pop Art.

Second, consider the titles of the two famous works of Heinz Edelmann, namely *Andromedar SR1* (text by Martin Ripkens and Hans Stempel, 1970) and *Maicki Astromaus* (text by Frederic Brown, 1970). The former title refers to a rocket called "Andromeda" whereas "SR1" is an abbreviation of "super rocket 1"; the title is explained in the text. The latter title had been suggested by the Austrian poet H. C. Artmann; "Astromaus" is sort of a translation of the original title of Fredric Brown's short story *The Star Mouse* (1941) (see Figure 1). The first name *Maicki*, of course, alludes to Mickey Mouse (or in German: Micky Maus), the famous mouse character created by Walt Disney.

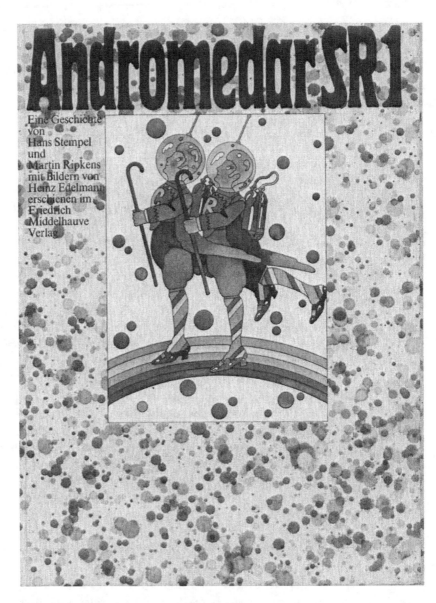

FIGURE 1 Book cover of *Andromedar SR1* with a text by Martin Ripkens and Hans Stempel, and illustrations by Heinz Edelmann. Köln: Friedrich Middelhauve Verlag, 1970 (color figure available online).

Third, we find baroque titles like *How the Mouse Was Hit on the Head by a Stone and So Discovered the World* (Etienne Delessert 1971), or *The Geranium on the Window Sill Just Died But Teacher You Went Right On* (Albert Cullum 1971). It goes without saying that the same titles rendering parts of the texts are atypical titles for picturebooks. They are too long, and may not easily be cited in discourse.

In summary, there are titles of Pop Art picturebooks that possess boundary-transgressing properties because of their allusional potential, complexity, or simply length.

Paratexts

The fact that boundaries exist with regard to the accessibility of the Pop Art picturebooks is reflected in paratexts accompanying some of the books. For instance, on the back cover of *Théo la Terreur* (Timothy the Terror 1972) by François Ruy-Vidal and Jean-Jacques Loup you can read:

> Attention! Attention! Attention!
> Such books could set children thinking, they could pose questions!

While persuading parents to run the risk of raising "curious" children is a quite aggressive strategy (this obviously being an aim of the anti-authoritarian movement), other books tend to explain their ideological background to the adults.

Thus, in *The Geranium on the Window Sill Just Died But Teacher You Went Right On* by Albert Cullum, dealing with the contrast between the authoritarian teacher and the sheer helplessness of the generic pupil, it is taken for granted that most of the adults have nightmarish memories of their school years, too: "The reader is stimulated to memorize and simultaneously reflect about possible experiences of the child—not in order to withhold them from herself and the child, but in order to talk to the child about these experiences and those of the child" (n.p.).

"Speaking with the child" is, of course, another aim of the anti-authoritarian movement, directed against the "speechlessness" of the parental generation. In *Mani das lügst du wieder* (Mani,

You Are Lying Again 1974) there is an explanation addressed to parents on how to deal with their lying children:

> Tips for parents:
>
> For children it is often hard to distinguish fantasy and reality. How should parents react to the fantastic stories of a child? Where does showing an understanding interest and a discourse between the big and the little one lead to? What is behind Mani's wildly proliferating story of the animal? Whoever looks at this book together with children, will—maybe—in future be more carefully with the assertion: That is another lie . . . (our translation)

Lying is, of course, a behavior that usually is punished by authoritarian parents. And, some of them certainly tend to expect a moral lesson from a "good" picturebook. Thus, in a separate sheet added to the German edition of *Le chat de Simulombula* (Simulombula's cat 1972) by Jacqueline Held, one reads:

> A story's moral does not exist here. And the pedagogical, moralizing undertone does not even come through the loophole. Everything goes mad and you can do a forward roll with your fantasy. The big, coloured pictures are no obstacle to this. Quite the contrary! Because persons and story are shown by three different artists (which are internationally well renowned), the reader and viewer is presented with a true range of opinions. (our translation)

The text does not propose any specific moral, but rather a definitely non-pedagogical offer is made which appeals to the imagination of the reader. Liberal parents are invited to form their own opinion, as do the international renowned artists.

Finally, this new anti-pedagogy is backed up by scientific authorities. For instance, the author of *The Geranium on the Window Sill Just Died But Teacher You Went Right On*, Albert Cullum, is explicitly introduced as an university teacher for early childhood education. Still more explicitly, the world-famous cognitive psychologist Jean Piaget contributes a preface for Etienne Delessert's *How the Mouse Was Hit on the Head by a Stone and So Discovered the World*. Here, Piaget points out that this book is partly a result of three interviews with 23 children aged 5 to 6 years. In the first part of the interview, children discussed pictures and stories from

Eugène Ionesco's and Etienne Delessert's *Story No 1,* and *Story No 2.* In the second part of the three interview sessions, the children were asked how they judged texts and pictures prepared by Etienne Delessert and psychologist Odile Mosmann. In the third part, children were asked to draw pictures themselves. All their responses were analyzed and influenced the final version of the book. For instance, children criticized words that were hard to understand, or they criticized mismatches between the narrative world and their own reality. Apart from the issue of impressing skeptical parents, an experimental approach to children's books where children may have the chance to influence the book, seems to be a revolutionary approach where cognitive psychology and children's literature meet.

A comment that is addressed to the child reader is added on a separate leaf to *Olivia kann fliegen* (Olivia Can Fly 1976) by Franz Buchrieser and illustrated by Erhard Göttlicher. Here it is explained how to use this—ambitious—story:

> The story of OLIVIA is not for being read again and again and again. This story is for butting in. You must read it with someone you like and who is clever, too. You must stop reading time and again, and interrupt, question and think often. This story is in no way finished. You can make it much more interesting yourself, if you write yourself into the story. This is exciting, try it sometimes! (our translation)

It is particularly interesting that this book originally appeared with the publisher *Bertelsmann,* but then was edited by the publisher *Grafik & Literatur.* In the same leaflet, this is explained to the child reader in the form of a little anti-capitalist story.

> One day, however, the big boss came into the children's literature department and said to the editors: "You are making books that are too complicated, books that children do not want to have. Children are not clever enough to deal with complicated stories." Then the big boss fired the editors of the children's literature department and the poets and painters too. The books already made he also did not want to sell. The boss had the opinion that foolish books were easier to sell and I want [sic] to have a full till with a lot of money in it. (Our translation)

We have shown, then, that boundaries of stories that are too complicated, or are an offense to traditional pedagogical values, are reflected in paratextual comments that are addressed to parents as well as children.

Discussion

The transfer of these unusual ideas to picturebooks reveals that the artists base their decision to create a Pop Art picturebook on a specific image of childhood which is often explained in the paratexts, that is, foreword, afterword, text insert, or blurb. These texts show that the authors or illustrators obviously rely on a concept of childhood that strongly holds to the idea that children have openness towards new experiences and ideas, while adults are often constrained by prejudices and biased opinions. Nevertheless, the preconditions for the reception of Pop Art are different. Children usually do not have the required world knowledge about mass communication, modern society, and politics, let alone drugs, advertisement, and the often quoted icons of pop culture. It appears then, that Pop Art picturebooks often touch adult perspectives and problems. The particular Pop Art format the artists choose, with respect to the texts as well as the pictures, is of course conditioned by their individual artistic focus or program.

It is our contention that "strangeness" should be considered as a new category or concept when dealing with the reception of children's books in general or picturebooks in particular. Evaluative adjectives like "strange," "peculiar," or "odd" are frequently used by children when they have problems with the judgment on or comprehensibility of stories and pictures (they even apply these categories to other items as well, but this is out of our specific discussion).

Under the precondition that "strangeness" is an adequate notion for this specific experience, one might assume that it should be applied to those children's books that definitively challenge the child audience in the following cases:

1. children are not able to refer to their world knowledge in order to grasp the sense of the text and/or illustrations;
2. neither text nor pictures support the child's developing sense of story, picture, or world knowledge;

3. the works in question do not observe the cognitive, emotional and aesthetic abilities of the age group for which the books are intended; and
4. regarding these developmental aspects, the respective books do not pay much attention to this important issue, but more or less exclusively stress the exceptional artistic and innovative concept of the work in question.

With regard to these options, the concept of "strangeness" is strongly linked to the question of the transgression of boundaries. What is, then, a boundary when considering cultural artifacts such as picturebooks?

We would like to suggest the following definition: Boundary is a cognitive, social, and aesthetic convention that refers to mutually accepted knowledge about the functions and meanings of pictures, text, and their relations. Transgressing boundaries aims at shifting these boundaries in order to extend the domain of mutually accepted knowledge with respect to these functions and meanings.

Or, as defined by cognitive psychology, already acquired schemata or scripts must be reinterpreted and revised by a bottom up/top down process, so that the new information rendered by text and/or pictures can be implemented, thus contributing to the existing scripts' or schemata's enrichment. In this regard, transgressing boundaries—whatever that comprises, whether it be cognitive, social, aesthetic, or emotional aspects—might be a demanding and satisfying experience for the child.

However, if the child cannot understand the picturebook's implied meaning and is therefore hindered in finding pleasure when looking at the pictures and reading/hearing the story, this transgressing process is certainly not unproblematic. A picturebook that expects too much of the child audience prevents a successful communication, even under the guidance of an adult mediator. As a result, children will usually lose interest in engaging with the book.

At least some Pop Art picturebooks, so we have argued, transgress the boundaries of the "good" picturebook. In order to flesh out that claim, we introduced the notion of a boundary. If that boundary is crossed, the result is strangeness. Admittedly, this is a pre-theoretical notion, but one which in our view deserves further exploration. Pop Art picturebooks are a promising field in that regard because of a wild mixture of artistic styles and complex (if not silly) stories. Surprisingly enough, there is very little research here. As a further speculation, we want to add that Pop Art picturebooks paved the way for the development of postmodern picturebooks in the 1980s and 1990s. Moreover, they appear to be cases of crosswriting in the realm of picturebooks, since many of their pictorial ideas and narrative contents appear to be targeted at an adult audience; therefore, they might be regarded as persuasive examples of "crossover picturebooks."

Picturebooks Cited

Andersen, Hans Christian. *Poucette*. Illus. Nicole Claveloux. Paris: Editions des femmes, 1978. Print.

Brown, Fredric. "Star Mouse" (first published 1941). In: Fredric Brown. *Space on My Hand*. New York: Bantam Books, 1951. Print.

Brown, Fredric. *Maicki Astromaus*. Illus. Heinz Edelmann. Translated by Uwe Friesel. Köln: Gertraud Middelhauve Verlag, 1970. Print.

Buchrieser, Franz.*Olivia kann fliegen*. Illus. Erhard Göttlicher. Hamburg, Graz: Grafik & Literatur, 1976. Print.

Carroll, Lewis: *Alice's Adventures in Wonderland*. London: Macmillan, 1865. Print.

Couratin, Patrick. *Herr Hut. Nicht Herr Mithut. Nicht Herr Ohnehut. Immer Herr Hut.* Told by Rolf Haufs. Köln: Gertraud Middelhauve Verlag, 1973. Print.

Couratin, Patrick. *Mister Bird*. New York: Harlin Quist, 1971. Print.

Cullum, Albert. *The Geranium on the Window Sill Just Died But Teacher You Went Right On*. Illus. various. New York: Harlin Quist, 1972. Print.

Delessert, Etienne. *How the Mouse Was Hit on the Head by a Stone and So Discovered the World*. New York: Doubleday, 1971. Print.

Held, Jacqueline. *Le chat de Simulombula*. Illus. Bernard Bonhomme, Nicole Claveloux, and Maurcie Garnier. Paris, New York: Harlin Quist, 1972. Print.

Held, Jaqueline. *Haltet den Kater, er hat den Frühling geklaut!* Illus. Bernard Bonhomme, Nicole Claveloux, and Maurice Garnier. Translated by Maja Inhauser. Aarau: Sauerländer, 1972. Print.

Hughes, Richard.*Gertrude and the Mermaid*. Illus. Nicole Claveloux. New York: Harlin Quist, 1971. Print.

Ionesco, Eugene. *Story Number 1*. Illus. Etienne Delessert. New York: Harlin Quist, 1968. Print.

Ionesco, Eugene. *Story Number 2*. Illus. Etienne Delessert. New York: Harlin Quist, 1971. Print.

Ionesco, Eugene. *Story Number 3*. Illus. Philippe Corentin. New York: Harlin Quist, 1971. Print.

Ionesco, Eugene. *Story Number 4*. Illus. Jean-Michel Nicollet. New York: Harlin Quist, 1973. Print.

Jägersberg, Otto. *Rüssel in Komikland*. Illus. Leo Leonhard. Darmstadt: Melzer Verlag, 1972. Print.

Max, Peter. *The Land of Yellow*. New York: Franklin Watts, 1970. Print.

Ripkens, Martin, and Hans Stempel. *Andromedar SR-1*. Illus. Heinz Edelmann. Köln: Friedrich Middelhauve Verlag, 1970. Print.

Ruy-Vidal, François, and Jean-Jacques Loup. *Théo la Terreur*. Paris, New York: Harlin Quist, 1972. Print.

Schmid, Eleonore. *The Endless Party*. Illus. Etienne Delessert. New York: Harlin Quist, 1967. Print.

Sendak, Maurice. *Where the Wild Things Are*. New York: Harper & Row, 1963. Print.

Steiner, Jörg. *Pele sein Bruder*. Illus. Werner Maurer. Köln: Gertraud Middelhauve Verlag, 1972. Print.

Van der Essen, Anne. *Yok-Yok*. Illus. Etienne Delessert. Köln: Gertraud Middelhauve Verlag, 1979 (English translation: *Blackbird and Three Other Stories: Yok Yok Series*. New York: Merrill Publ., 1980). Print.

Walbert, Helmut. *Mani das lügst du wieder*. Illus. Klaus Endrikat. Ravensburg: Otto Maier Verlag, 1974. Print.

Yellow Submarine. Director: George Dunning. United Kingdom/USA: Apple Films, 1968.

References

Alloway, Lawrence. "Popular Culture and Pop Art." *Pop Art. A Critical History*. Ed. Steven Henry Madoff. Berkeley: University of California Press, 1997. 167–174 first published in 1969). Print.

Bader, Barbara. *American Picturebooks from Noah's Ark to the Beast Within*. New York: Macmillan, 1976. Print.

Kiefer, Barbara Z. *The Potential of Picturebooks. From Visual Literacy to Aesthetic Understanding*. Englewood-Cliffs: Prentice Hall, 1995. Print.

Künnemann, Horst. "Zur Gegenwartssituation." *Das Bilderbuch. Geschichte und Entwicklung des Bilderbuchs in Deutschland von den Anfängen bis zur Gegenwart*. Eds. Klaus Doderer, and Helmut Müller. Weinheim/Basel: Beltz, 1973. 395–436. Print.

Nikolajeva, Maria, and Carole Scott. *How Picturebooks Work*. New York/London: Garland, 2001. Print.

Nodelman, Perry. *Words About Pictures. The Narrative Art of Children's Picture Books*. Athens: University of Georgia Press, 1988. Print.

Thiele, Jens. "Pop-up, pop-down. Bildnerische Reflexionen der Populärkultur im Bilderbuch." *Populär. Popliteratur und Jugendkultur*. Ed. Johannes G. Pankau. Bremen: Asch, 2004. 177–186. Print.

BEFORE AND AFTER THE PICTUREBOOK FRAME:
A TYPOLOGY OF ENDPAPERS

TERESA DURAN and EMMA BOSCH

Department of Teacher Training in Visual and Plastic Arts, University of
Barcelona, Barcelona, Spain

*The original reason for having endpapers in books was purely practical, one
of the technical requirements of the binding process. From the 1960s, however,
graphic designers working on picturebooks played a decisive role in changing
this function when they began to use endpapers for communicative purposes.
Picturebooks are conceived as the product of an overall design in which each
part of the book serves the story. The endpapers, which are found in a privileged
position at the very beginning and at the end of the book, have come to be seen by
many authors and publishers as an ideal place for these communicative purposes.
This article presents a typology of endpapers based on how they relate to the story
and the form in which they appear. Our aim is for researchers, specialists, and
readers to stop thinking of the picturebook simply as an illustrated book and to
pay more attention to all of its separate parts, any of which may contain valuable
information for interpreting the story.*

Endpapers are sheets of paper glued to book covers in order
to secure them to the text block. As a part of the technical
requirements of the binding process, their main function is purely
practical and they are an essential part of hardcover books.
Craftsmen originally made them one at a time. Under the influence of William Morris, artists began to illustrate them with
geometric and floral designs. Children's books published during the 1920s contain beautiful examples of illustrated endpapers
which aimed to attract the attention of younger readers. The role
of graphic designers in creating picturebooks was decisive from
the 1960s onwards - they saw the creation of these books as an
all-encompassing design and began to pay special attention to the

endpapers, giving them an importance exceeding their practical functionality.

In this article, we aim to show that, due to their privileged position before and after the story, endpapers can have a very important function as regards meaning and narrative. We also wanted to create an endpaper typology based on the type of function they had in picturebooks. Certain specialists have touched on the narrative role of endpapers, but we had not previously come across any typological study of them until the recent publication by Sipe and McGuire (2009). They also point out that picturebook specialists have not paid as much attention to endpapers as they should have, and that they were therefore presenting a typology.

Following the terminology coined by Genette (1987), Sipe and McGuire (2009) consider endpapers to be one of the most important paratexts of the picturebook in that they can complement the content of the book, the "text." Genette defines paratexts as any verbal or non-verbal productions that surround, prolong, present, and give presence to the text, for example, the author's name, the title, the preface, and illustrations. Genette distinguishes between author and publisher paratexts depending on what source they come from. Depending on their physical situation, he differentiates between *peritexts*, if they can be found in the actual space of the volume (chapter titles, notes, preface . . .), and *epitexts*, if the messages can be found outside the book (interviews, personal diaries, preambles, adverts, reviews . . .).

Many authors, including ourselves, agree that in picturebooks "everything counts": the jacket, the flyleaf, the title pages . . . Every part of the book can serve the narrative, and indeed this is what often happens. If all the physical spaces of the picturebook can be used for narrative purposes, then perhaps it is no longer appropriate to distinguish between "text" and "paratexts." Our opinion is that this terminology is no longer appropriate in the study of picturebooks because the "text" is much more than just a written story. Neither the jacket nor the endpapers nor the title pages can be considered paratexts in many picturebooks because all those spaces may contain "text." Strictly speaking they are the "text."

Sipe and McGuire (2009) classify endpapers into four categories. Their typology is based on a mixture of two facets: on the one hand depending on the content of the endpapers—whether they are plain or illustrated—and on the other depending on the relationship between the front and back endpapers—whether they are identical or not. Hence the following groups are obtained: plain and identical, plain and different, illustrated and identical, illustrated and different.

Our classification is more complex, structured according to the endpapers' function in the context of the story. In the first subdivision—adopting the terminology coined by Genette (1987), although in a slightly different sense—we make a distinction between those endpapers that have an exogenous relationship with the text (epitextual) and those that have an endogenous relationship (peritextual).

Epitextual endpapers are those which make some sort of allusion to the collection or to the publisher; make some reference to the author; contain dedications or tributes, or are directed explicitly to the reader. In other words, all those where the content is not closely and significantly related to the narrative.

In *peritextual* endpapers the content interacts with the story. This group contains any endpapers that introduce the characters; show where the narrative takes place or the theme of the story; make use of the space to start or end the story; and also those containing games or additional information relating to the content of the book.

Some of these categories can be subdivided on a secondary level according to form. Sipe and McGuire (2009) present two types of endpaper based on this idea, making a distinction between plain and illustrated. We subdivide into three groups: plain, patterned, and illustrated. Plain endpapers are those of a single homogeneous color; patterned endpapers are made up of graphic elements rhythmically repeated following a pattern occupying the entire area; and illustrated endpapers include an illustration that is not organized in modular form.

Before we move on to our classification, we should point out that there are some endpapers that have no special significance, no particular purpose, and that contain nothing that can be appreciated on anything other than a practical level, and which we therefore cannot include in any of the subsections we have established. The color of some plain endpapers may have been chosen with no communicative intention. However, color is seldom a random choice. The decision tends to be made with the aim of establishing overall aesthetic consistency. A particular shade may be used because it is the same as that used on the jacket or because it is one of the predominant colors used for the illustrations inside the book. The endpapers of *Big Sister, Little Sister* (2005) by Leuyen Pham, for example, have been designed with a striped pattern combining ochres, pinks, greens, and whites, which are the colors used to illustrate the book.

Endpaper Typology

Before we present our typology, we would like to mention that we were surprised in the course of our study to find that some translations have not retained the design of the original endpapers. One example of this can be found in Raymond Briggs's book *The Snowman*. In the French and Italian editions the endpapers are white, but in the Catalonian edition they are silver. In order to avoid confusion, in cases where we have not had access to the original book, we will specify which edition we consulted (if there is an English translation we add the title in italics; if not, we simply add a literal translation). The original titles can be found in the bibliography.

1. Endpapers with Epitextual Content in Relation to the Story
   1.1 Collection, Series, or Publisher
   1.2 Author
   1.3 Dedications and Tributes
   1.4 Reader

1.1 Collection, Series, or Publisher

Some publishers use a specific design for their collections. The use of the same basic color and/or typographic codes on both the outside and the inside of the book makes it clear that the book belongs to a particular collection. These graphic resources can also be used to identify a series or even a publisher. The endpapers are often used as an element serving to identify a collection, series, or publisher.

Plain: All the books in the *Sin palabras* (Without words) collection published by La Galera have plain endpapers, although the colors vary across the different books that make up the collection.

Patterned: An interesting example of a patterned endpaper identifying a series of books can be found in *Die Torte ist weg* (*Where is the Cake?*) by Thé Tjong Khing. The endpapers in the first volume are designed with a pattern of cakes, the same cakes as the one the book's characters look for. In the second volume *Picknick mit Torte* (*Where is the Cake Now?*), the pattern is composed of a great many pairs of cakes. There is a twofold meaning to this pattern; on the one hand it is because two cakes have disappeared in this book, and on the other it confirms that this is the second part of the story (See Figure 1). Should there be a new adventure, we look forward to discovering whether it will deal with the search for three missing cakes and whether the pattern on the endpapers will show trios of cakes.

Illustrated: The Constance and Tiny collection of picturebooks written by Pierre Le Gall and illustrated by Eric Héliot, published in Spain by Edelvives also has graphically coded endpapers. We find the same illustration in all the books but with a different background color for each volume, the same shade as the cover illustration. Hence, *Carlota y Miniatura* (*Constance and Tiny*) shows the faces of the cat and the main character

FIGURE 1 Endpapers of *Picknick mit Torte* by Thé Tjong-Khing (color figure available online).

on a grey background, *Carlota y los piratas* (Constance and the Pirates) on a sky blue background, and *Carlota en el internado* (*Constance and the Great Escape*) on a pale pink background. The design brings the three volumes together as parts of a series and differentiates between them using a color code. The endpapers of the "Contes d'arreu" (Tales from all over) collection of folk tales published by Publicacions de l'Abadia de Montserrat are a good example of collection design. Each volume in the series has different endpapers, but they all make some sort of reference to the culture from which the story comes. The Indian tale *Compta fins a cinc* (Count to five), illustrated by Sebastià Serra, shows a sari, whereas the story from India - *El còndor i les estrelles* (The condor and the stars), illustrated by Lluís Ferrer, shows a motif from Inca ceramics.

1.2 Author

The endpapers can be a good place to refer in some way to the author. A brief biography or a list of other books from the same publisher may appear along with the author's photograph. An example that refers to the author in the form of publicity can be found in the final endpapers of *L'Orage* (The Storm), which states "Bibliographie: Anne Brouillard, l'un des très grands talents de cette décennie, a déjà publié chez Grandir *Le Voyage*, en 1984, toujours disponible".[1]

1.3 Dedications and Tributes

Although it is not usual to use the endpaper page as a courtesy page, the space can be used by the author to dedicate the book to someone or write a tribute. One outstanding example among the few we have found is the text of the tribute to the Merghic Realm that Jackie Morris writes on the endpapers of *The Snow Leopard*, in which she praises the peaceful inhabitants of the highest mountains in the world, who live in harmonious communication with the spirits of the mountains and high pastures (See Figure 2).

---

[1]Bibliography: Anne Brouillard, one of the great talents of the decade, is also the author of *Le Voyage*, published by Grandir in 1984 and still available.

FIGURE 2 Endpapers of *The Snow Leopard* by Jackie Morris (color figure available online).

1.4 Reader

The endpapers are the perfect place for readers to write their names as an act of taking possession of the picturebook. We refer to the type of text that says "This book belongs to . . .". In the German version of *The Idle Bear* by Robert Ingpen (*Teddybären unter sich*), alongside an illustration of a large teddy bear there is a space reserved for readers to enter their names underneath the phrase "This book belongs to the teddy bears' friend . . .". This is a lovely way of involving the reader in the story (see Figure 3).

2. Endpapers with Peritextual Content in Relation to the Story
   2.1 Characters
   2.2 Location
   2.3 Theme
   2.4 Preface and Epilogue
   2.5 Bonus Track

FIGURE 3 Endpapers of *Teddybären unter sich* by Robert Ingpen (color figure available online).

2.1   Characters

The main and/or secondary characters are commonly found on the endpapers of picturebooks. Introducing the characters is a very common way of beginning a story, and let us not forget that the initial endpapers are at the start of the book, at the very beginning of the story.

Plain: The color used for plain endpapers can be a reference to the main character in the story. The shade of pink chosen by Geisert for the endpapers of *Oink* (*Oink*), for instance, is the same color as the pigs that appear in the story. In fact this picture book is printed in two shades of ink (black and pink). In *La merienda del señor Verde* (Mr Green's Tea), Javier Sáez Castán has used a monochrome green background for the endpapers. Although the green is connected to the main character in the story, it can also be related to Señor Verde's surroundings since his entire world is that color.

Patterned: Books aimed at younger readers tend to have different depictions of the characters appearing in the story. In this way it becomes easier to identify the characters and in turn enables the reader to identify with them. The endpapers of *The Funny Thing* by Wanda Gág are made up of a modular composition of the main characters. The classical impression is obtained by showing these characters framed in lockets. Leo Lionni also introduces his characters on the endpapers of *Pequeño Azul y Pequeño Amarillo* (*Little Blue and Little Yellow*), filling the entire surface with blue and yellow dots, which are the leading players in this story. Ann and Paul Rand show off their talent for graphics on the endpapers of *El pequeño 1* (*Little 1*) with a simple, subtle pattern of small orange 1s on a white background (see Figure 4).

Illustrated: An example of endpapers, which at first glance may appear to be patterned, can be found in *Tomppa* (*Our tommy*) by Kristiina Louhi. If we look more closely we can see that all the babies are different (some are sitting, some are crawling . . .). Geoffroy de Pennart also uses the endpapers to introduce the main characters in *Le Loup est revenu* (The Wolf is Back!). The illustrator has created a nighttime scene in which the wolf is creeping menacingly toward the lights of the rabbit's little house.

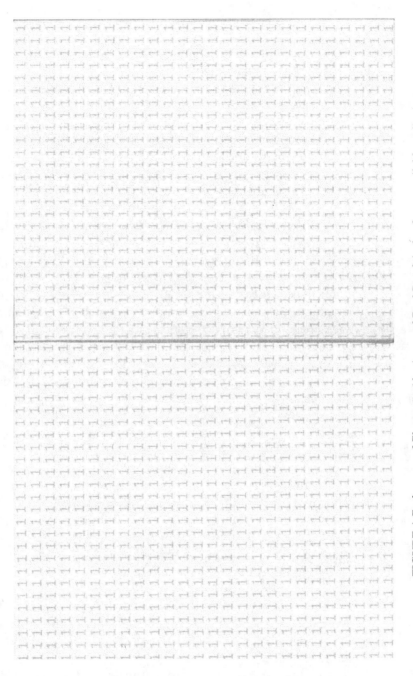

FIGURE 4 Endpapers of *El pequeño 1* by Ann and Paul Rand (color figure available online).

2.2 Location

The endpapers in some picturebooks carry out the function of helping the reader to locate the story.

Plain: We can see an example of this type of endpaper in the book *Une soirée au théâtre avec Mr Catastrophe* (*Paddy's Evening Out*), by J. S. Goodall, the red color of which alludes to the curtain of the theatre in which Mr. Catastrophe wreaks havoc.

Patterned: The endpapers patterned with bath tiles in the picturebook *La puerta* (The Door) by Michel Van Zeveren let us know how important this place—the bathroom—will be in the story of a little pig who yearns to have a bath in private.

Illustrated: In *Elsa y Max de paseo por París* (*Adèle & Simon*), Barbara McClintock shows us a map of Paris on the opening endpapers, with the route the characters will take on this walk marked with a blue line. On the closing endpapers, as well as the map there is a key to the exact places where Max/Simon has lost his belongings (see Figure 5). *Madlenka* by Peter Sís helps us locate the action thanks to a zoom effect which starts on the endpapers and shows two images of the Earth, the second one showing the location of New York City. The author uses the same strategy in *El muro (The Wall)*, this time showing Prague, the city in which the story takes place.

2.3 Theme

The theme of the book can also be shown on the endpapers.

Plain: What color would the endpapers be of a book dealing with the fear of going to sleep in the dark be? Black, of course! And that is precisely the colour of the endpapers in *Licht aus!* (*Lights Out*), a book by Arthur Geisert which describes the complicated contraption the main character has invented to delay the switching-off of his bedside table lamp.

The yellow endpapers in *El niño estrella* (*The Little Boy Star: An Allegory of the Holocaust*) by Olivier Latyk are the same color as the star that the Jewish boy, the main character of this story about the Holocaust written by Rachel Hausfater, has to wear sewn onto his clothes.

Patterned: The stamps that appear on the endpapers of *Tokio* (Tokyo) by Taro Miura are a link to the postcards the main

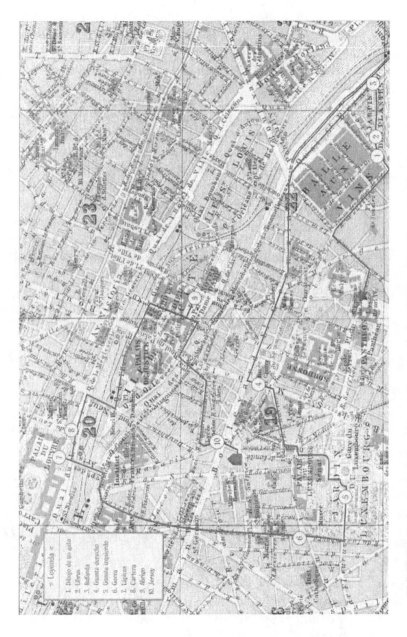

FIGURE 5 Endpapers of *Elsa y Max de Paseo por París* by Barbara McClintock (color figure available online).

character sends to her friends during her trip to this Japanese city. The pattern of naked bodies with sexual attributes in *Zizis et zézettes* (Peas & Butterflies), a story of boys and girls who discover their sexuality, illustrated by Vittoria Facchini, are also a link to the theme of the book. Elwood H. Smith illustrates the endpapers of *Raise the Roof!* with the tools the characters use to repair the roof in the story.

Illustrated: One illustration which focuses perfectly on the theme of the picturebook can be found in *Ich bin für mich* (Vote for me!) by Martin Baltscheit, where the illustrator Christine Schwarz draws an advertising hoarding showing posters of all the candidates in the presidential election. This funny, tongue-in-cheek political campaign in the animal kingdom is the theme of this particular picturebook (see Figure 6). Another example would be the picturebook by Paul Maar, *El viaje de Lisa* (Lisa's Travel), in which the illustrator Kestutis Kasparavicius shows a number of different pillows floating against a white background, alluding to the world of dreams through which the main character travels. We notice that the author includes his signature in the pattern, proclaiming his authorship with great professional zeal.

2.4   Preface and Epilogue

The privileged position of the endpapers at the beginning and end of the book can be used for narrative purposes. The endpapers at the beginning can show the situation as it was before the story takes place, and then the endpapers at the end can reveal to us how this situation has changed due to the events that take place in the book. The endpapers therefore act both as the story's preface and epilogue.

Patterned: An example can be found in *L'ennemi* (*The Enemy*), by Davide Cali and Serge Bloch, the endpapers of which are sufficiently explicit to show the content of the picturebook in just two images. The preface is not limited to the confines of a single page but is developed over eight pages before it reaches the title page.

Illustrated: In *El millor Nadal* (*The Best Christmas Ever*) the author, Chih-Yuan Chen, shows a "before and after" situation for the story. It is the same illustration of the building's courtyard, but there is a different detail on the window: the snowman and the

FIGURE 6 Endpapers of *Ich bin für mich* by Martin Baltscheit and Christine Schwarz (color figure available online).

Christmas items that decorate it reveal that, in the end and despite everything, the family has been able to have a happy Christmas. *Roule ma poule* (Roll My Chicken) by Elisabeth Brami and Claude Cachin is a picturebook with verses presenting a metaphorical parallel between a circus show and a lifecycle from before birth to death. On the opening endpapers we see the circus ring lit up and a little toy hen on the point of entering it, while the closing endpapers show the spotlights switched off and the little toy hen on its side (see Figures 7a and 7b). Neil Curtis in *Gat i Peix* (*Cat and Fish*) shows the main characters before and after the story. On the endpapers at the front Cat and Fish do not know each other and do not even look at each other—the fish is swimming and the cat, on a bridge, is looking elsewhere. At the end, after they both decide to run away in the story, the endpapers show them flying over the sea together. We would like to highlight the ingenious metafictional use of the endpapers in *El apestoso hombre queso y otros cuentos maravillosamente estúpidos* (*The Stinky Cheeseman and Other Fairly Stupid Tales*) by Jon Scieszka and Lane Smith, in which the appearance of the final endpaper well before the end of the story confuses the characters and gives rise to a number of jokes because of a supposedly deliberate "mistake."

2.5   Bonus Track

In musical terms, a *bonus track* refers to an extra song added to the album. We have borrowed the term to refer to those endpapers which the authors have used to add a game or information surplus to the story itself, something that could be considered an appendix, a "gift" from the authors.

Patterned: Steven Guarnaccia adds some extra information to the story of Goldilocks on the endpapers of *Boucle d'Or et les Trois Ours* (*Goldilocks and the Three Bears: A Modern Tale*). As if it were a catalogue, he gives an inventory of the objects and pieces of furniture that appeared in the three bears' house. The odd thing about this is that the objects are very well-known pieces in the fields of industrial and interior design, and therefore, as well as the image, the author includes the designer's name, the country, the name of the piece and the date it was made, thereby creating an interesting encyclopedia-style catalogue (See Figure 8).

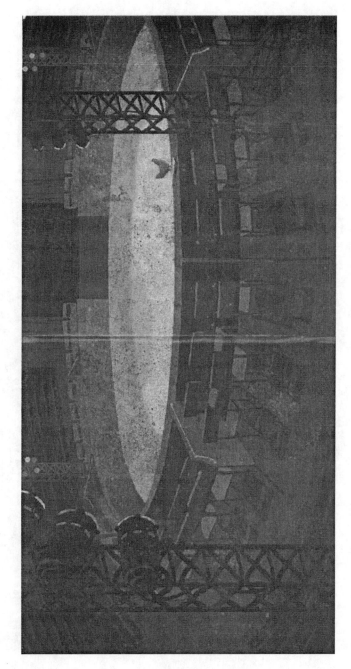

FIGURE 7a Opening endpapers of *Roule ma poule* by Elisabeth Brami and Claude Cachin (color figure available online).

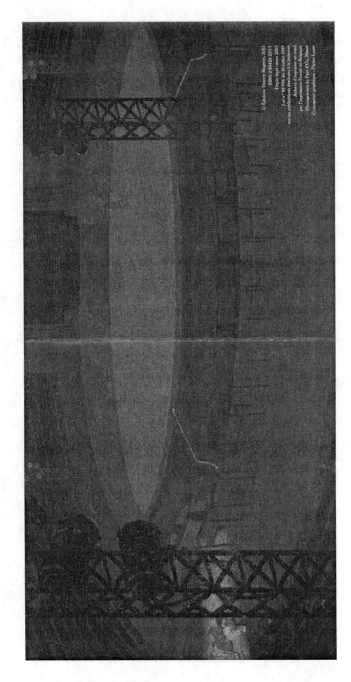

FIGURE 7b Closing endpapers of *Roule ma poule* by Elisabeth Brami and Claude Cachin (color figure available online).

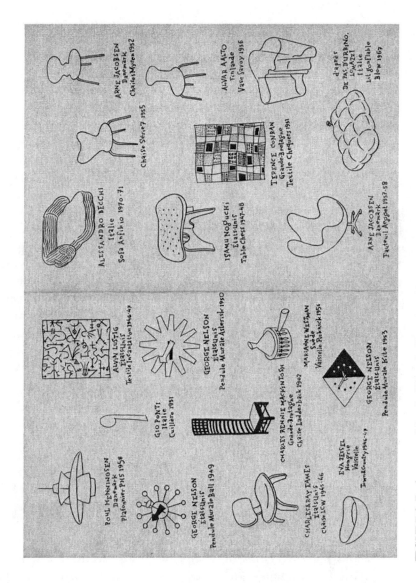

FIGURE 8 Endpapers of *Boude d'Or et les Trois Ours* by Steven Guarnaccia (color figure available online).

In *Adivina quién hace qué. Un paseo invisible* (Guess Who Does What! An Invisible Walk) by Gerda Müller, the front and back endpapers are identical. The author has designed a pattern using the main characters in the story—a boy and a dog—showing them in different positions that help us to understand the actions that made the tracks we have had to follow during this story without words. It is the solution to the reading game involved in the book, additional information that complements the story but it is not essential.

Illustrated: On the endpapers at the back of *El viaje de Max* (*Max's Travel*) by Gauthier and Caudry, an interesting game has been prepared which readers could miss if they do not read the story carefully. There are a number of illustrations like small post-cards hanging on the wall of the main character's cabin. They are fragments of the illustrations inside the book which the reader has to find. Hence the readers discover a parallel world which might otherwise have passed them by without them realizing it. Finally, although it concerns a book of knowledge, we love the endpapers in *Le livre de la mer* (The Book of the Sea), written by Silvie Baussier and illustrated by Climent Devaux, which provide us with a little entertainment, a two-scene cartoon. The endpapers at the front of the book show a sea dragon chasing a little blue fish, while the final endpapers show the little blue fish—which we now identify as an extremely dangerous piranha—chasing the sea dragon that swims away terrified.

Conclusions

To summarize, our examination of some of the properties of endpapers, which began simply out of curiosity, ended up showing that it was possible for us to group them along certain basic typo-logical lines. What in the beginning was only a random sample took on shape and depth and, although some of the typological categories we outline seem to be larger than others, at least in our personal collections, this has not prevented us from discover-ing that we had enough—more than enough—examples for each category to confirm the viability of a field of research hitherto virtually unexplored.

Now that they have well and truly exceeded their merely prac-tical function in binding the picturebook, endpapers provide the illustrator with the perfect space to experiment with graphics, experiments that have explored new and ingenious paths over the years.

We would just like to add that some of the endpapers we have used as examples in one category could also be included in others depending on the interpretation or function prioritized. We would no doubt agree with any possible objections that readers of this article may make, but we would like to say that our intention here is not to put the endpapers into different categories but to learn how to observe them carefully and appreciate them and read them as another element of communication.

Although we have outlined four epitextual and five peritextual types of endpaper, we do not believe this exhausts all possibilities. No doubt the future will bring us new surprises and new categories, such as those offered by Ian Falconer's picturebook *Olivia . . . i la joguina perduda (Olivia . . . and the Missing Toy)*, where the relationship between the story's two characters is resolved via an ingenious sequence of twelve drawings without words. This picture narrative within the graphic narrative of the picturebook is actually included in the endpapers. For the present we consider it to be an unusual case. But there will be more, we can be sure of that. At least we hope so . . .

References

Genette, G. *Umbrales.* 1987. Mexico/Argentina: Siglo XXI Editores, 2006. Print.
Sipe, L., and C. McGuire. "Picture endpapers. Resources for literary and aesthetic interpretation." *Talking Beyond the Page: Reading and Responding to Picturebooks.* Ed. J. Evans. London/New York: Routledge, 2009. Print.

Children's Picturebooks Cited

Baltscheit, M. *Ich bin für mich.* Illus. C. Schwarz. Zurich: Bajazzo, 2005. Print.
Baussier, S. *Le livre de la mer.* Illus. C. Devaux. Paris: Nathan, 2005. Print.
Brami, E. *Roule ma poule.* Illus. C. Cachin. Paris: Thierry Magnier, 2003. Print.
Briggs, R. *El ninot de neu.* Barcelona: La Galera, 2007. (The Snowman, 1978). Print.
—. *Il pupazzo di neve.* Milan: Emme, 1980. (*The Snowman*, 1978).
—. *Le Bonhomme de neige.* Paris: Grasset & Fasquelle, 2005. (*The Snowman*, 1978). Print.

Brouillard, A. *L'Orage*. Nîmes: Grandir. 1998. Print.

Cali, D. *El enemigo*. Illus. S. Bloch. Madrid: SM, 2008. (*L'Ennemi*, 2007). Print.

Chen, C. Y. *El millor Nadal*. Barcelona: Thule, 2006. (*The Best Christmas Ever*, 2005). Print.

Curtis, N. *Gat i Peix*. Madrid: Los libros del zorro rojo, 2005. (*Cat and Fish*, 2005). Print.

De Pennart, G. *Le loup est revenu*. Paris: Kaléidoskope, 1994. Print.

Facchini, V. *Zizis et zézettes*. Paris: Circonflexe, 2000. (*Piselli e Farfalline . . . Son più belli i maschi o le bambine?*, 1999). Print.

Falconer, I. *Olivia . . . i la joguina perduda*. Mexico: FCE, 2004. (*Olivia . . . and the Missing Toy*, 2004). Print.

Gág, W. *The Funny Thing*. Minneapolis: University of Minnesota Press, 2003. Print.

Gauthier, D. *El viaje de Max*. Illus. M. Caudry. Barcelona: El Aleph, 2008. (*La balade de Max*, 2007). Print.

Geisert, A. *Licht aus!* Gestenberg: Gestenberg Verlag, 2006. (*Lights Out*, 2005). Print.

—. *Oink*. Mexico: Fondo de Cultura Económica, 1992. (*Oink*, 1991). Print.

Girona, R. *Compta fins a cinc*. Illus. S. Serra. Barcelona: Publicacions de l'Abadia de Montserrat, 2003. Print.

—. *El còndor i les estrelles*. Illus. L. Farré. Barcelona: Publicacions de l'Abadia de Montserrat, 2003. Print.

Goodall, J. S. *Une soirée au théâtre avec Mr Catastrophe*. Paris: Gallimard, 1979. (*Paddy's Evening Out*, 1973). Print.

Guarnaccia, S. *Boucle d'Or et les Trois Ours*. Paris: Seuil, 1999. (*Goldilocks and the Three Bears. A Modern Tale*, 1998). Print.

Hausfater, R. *El niño estrella*. Illus. O. Latyk. Madrid: Edelvives, 2001. (*L'enfant à l'étoile*, 2001). Print.

Ingpen, R. *Teddybären unter sich*. Münster: Coppenrath. 1987. (*The Idle Bear*, 1986). Print.

Maar, P. *El viaje de Lisa*. Illus. K. Kasparavicius. Mexico: FCE, 2004. (*Lisas Reise*, 1996). Print.

Lionni, L. *Pequeño Azul y Pequeño Amarillo*. Seville: Kalandraka. 2006. (*Little Blue and Little Yellow*, 1959). Print.

Le Gall, P. *Carlota en el internado*. Illus. E. Héliot. Madrid: Edelvives, 2008. (*Constance en pension*, 2008). Print.

—. *Carlota y los piratas*. Madrid: Edelvives, 2008. (*Constance et les pirates*, 2008). Print.

—. *Carlota y Miniatura*. Madrid: Edelvives, 2008. (*Constance et Miniature*, 2008). Print.

Louhi, K. *Meidän Tomppa*. Tampere (Finland): Tammi, 1993. Print.

McClintock, B. *Elsa y Max de paseo por París*. Barcelona: RBA, 2007. (*Adele and Simon*, 2006). Print.

Miura, T. *Tokio*. Valencia: Mediavaca. 2006. Print.

Morris, J. *The Snow Leopard*. London: Frances Lincoln Children's Book. 2007. Print.

Müller, G. *Adivina quién hace qué. Un paseo invisible*. Barcelona: Corimbo, 2001. (*Devine qui fait quoi*, 1999). Print.

Pham, L. *Big Sister, Little Sister*. New York: Hyperion Books, 2005. Print.

Rand, A. *El pequeño 1*. Illus. P. Rand. [Granada]: Barbara Fiore Editora. 2006. (Little 1, 1962). Print.

Sáez Castán, J. *La merienda del señor verde*. Caracas: Ekaré. 2007. Print.

Sís, P. *Madlenka*. Barcelona: Lumen, 2002. (*Madlenka*, 2000). Print.

—. *El muro*. Barcelona: Norma Editorial, 2009. (*The Wall*, 2007). Print.

Smith, E. H. *Raise the Roof!* Auckland (New Zealand): Penguin Books, 2003. Print.

Smith, L. *El apestoso hombre queso y otros cuentos maravillosamente estúpidos*. Illus. J. Scieszka. Barcelona: Thule, 2004. (*The Stinky Cheese Man*, 1992). Print.

Tjong-Khing, T. *Die Torte ist weg*. Barcelona: Art Blume, 2006. Print. (*War is de taart*, 2004).

—. *Picknick mit Torte*. Frankfurt am Main: Moritz Verlag, 2008. (*Picknick met taart*, 2005). Print.

Van Zeveren, M. *La puerta*. Barcelona: Corimbo, 2008. (*La porte*, 2008). Print.

"MUST WE TO BED INDEED?" BEDS AS CULTURAL SIGNIFIERS IN PICTUREBOOKS FOR CHILDREN

MARIA NIKOLAJEVA and LIZ TAYLOR

Faculty of Education, University of Cambridge, Cambridge, UK

The materiality as a characteristic feature of the picturebook does not only imply its existence as an artifact, but also its ability to represent a material world through images in a more direct and immediate manner than verbal texts. This article considers the representation of beds in picturebooks from two discreet yet closely connected perspectives: semiotics and cultural geography. The concept of place and space in a broad sense is central for the argument. Beds constitute a young child's closest surroundings and are frequently the only private space available. At the same time, beds are areas of power struggle between child and adult, as well as a border between self and the world, private and public. The article discusses, first, the physical aspects of the represented objects: their form, size, position on the page, and spatial relationship to other objects and characters, which all create a sense of space. Second, it probes into the function of the objects, such as their cultural connotations, significance for the narrative, and metaphorical implications.

Must we to bed indeed? Well then,
Let us arise and go like men,
And face with an undaunted tread
The long black passage up to bed.
(R. L. Stevenson, A Child's Garden of Verses)

The materiality as a characteristic feature of the picturebook does not only imply its existence as an artifact, but also its ability to represent a material world through images in a more direct and immediate manner than verbal texts. While a novel can offer a lengthy and detailed description of settings, images can convey an instant sense of environment, at the same time leaving gaps to encourage the viewers' imagination. It is enticing to consider, from several perspectives, material objects recurrent in the visual worlds of picturebooks and constituting a young child's closest surroundings, such as beds, tables, or bathrooms. On closer inspection, beds alone prove more than enough for a short paper. This article examines the representation of beds in children's picturebooks from two discreet yet closely connected perspectives: semiotics and cultural geography. The concept of place and space in a broad sense is central for the argument. Beds constitute a young child's closest surroundings and are frequently the only private space available. At the same time, beds are areas of power struggle between child and adult, as well as a border between self and the world, private and public. While bedroom scenes in picturebooks have been studied, for instance, by William Moebius (1991), Mary Galbraight (1999), Nina Goga (2010), and Ellen Spitz (1999, 23–75), these scholars focused on the psychological aspects of bedtime situations. Maria Tatar provides a fascinating social background to bedtime storytelling (2009, 41–50). In contrast, we will discuss, first, the physical, mimetic aspects of the objects: their form, size, position on the page, and spatial relationship to other objects and characters, which all create a sense of space. Second, we will probe into the function of the objects, such as their cultural connotations, significance for the narrative, and metaphorical implications.

Let us start with some simple considerations of how beds (or any other material objects) can be represented through verbal and visual media. Joseph Kosuth's famous work of art, *One and Three Chairs* (1965), on display at the Museum of Modern Art, New York, is an excellent example: an actual, three-dimensional object, a visual image and a dictionary definition of the word "chair." Art critics connect this conceptual piece to the semiotic theory of C. S. Peirce. In Peircian semiotics, each sign has a tripartite structure, the object (referent, signified), the sign (signifier) and the interpretant, that is, an individual's understanding of the relationship between the two (Peirce 1994). There are further three types of signs, depending on the relationships between the three constituents: icon, index, and symbol. An icon is connected to its referent by similarity. In other words, a bed must be recognizable as a bed. When we see images of beds in picturebooks, we normally correlate them with our abstract concept of bed-ness because the images have referents in the material world. However, this seemingly simple concept is culturally and historically dependent. What constitutes bed-ness? What is the material form of the object we would without hesitation call a bed? Some definitions one would find in internet sources include: "a piece of furniture that provides a place to sleep"; "a piece of furniture for reclining and sleeping, typically consisting of a flat, rectangular frame and a mattress resting on springs." These verbal indexical signs point at ("indicate") and evoke a concept of bed-ness. Obviously, beds look different throughout history and in different cultures. When Jesus says to the sick man: "Rise, take up thy bed, and walk" (John 5:8), presumably bedding rather than a frame is referred to. Yet the iconography of the bed in picturebooks is strikingly homogeneous. In our sample of about sixty Western picturebooks, mostly late twentieth and twenty-first century, bed-ness is tangibly emphasized through indicative features such as headboard, footboard, and traditional bedding. Even though very few modern children's beds actually look like that, it seems that bed-ness in picturebooks must necessarily be expressed through highly traditional, not to say obsolete images. The recognition does not address the familiar material object in the real world, but a representation known from previous textual experiences, a second-degree representation. It is quite remarkable that even twenty-first century illustrators apparently feel compelled to employ these outdated representations; however, it complies with the general trend in children's literature to depict the material and social world of the past even when the declared setting is present. If children's literature, as it is repeatedly maintained, is primarily an educational implement, the epistemic value of bed images is dubious.

Further, a bed as a semiotic sign may refer to a sleeping place rather than a piece of furniture, a function rather than an object: a place or article used by a person or animal for sleep or rest; or any place used for sleeping or reclining. A visual image of a bed can thus be also interpreted as an index, a sign that points at its referent. A road sign with an image of a bed usually indicates a hotel. An image of a bed in a picturebook indicates bedroom or nursery, that is, not merely a piece of furniture, but a particular space—and, one might add, a particular time, a chronotope.

Lastly, a symbol, in Peircian terms, is a sign connected to its referent by convention. While the image of a bed would normally work as an icon, on the symbolic level it may imply such notions as rest, peace, and relaxation. Reading in bed is a recurrent image in picturebooks, typically conveying a sense of security and tranquility, signifying a private space that fully belongs to the child, where the child also has control. In the images, the companions allowed to share the space with the child are dolls or soft toys.

On the other hand, a bed can signify old age (grandparents in bed) or sickness. The sickbed as a physical space, for instance in Ludwig Bemelmans' *Madeline* (1939), literally impedes the child's mobility, but eventually turns out to be a source of celebration, when the girl's surgery is successful, and even envy, since she is getting so much attention:

> in they walked and then said, "Ahhh,"
> when they say the toys and candy
> and the dollhouse from Papa.
> But the biggest surprise by far -
> *on her stomach*
> *was a scar!*

The cultural geographer Doreen Massey uses the idea of space as a "bundle of trajectories" to highlight the way in which the living and non-living parts that make up a place have come from somewhere and are on the way to somewhere else, over a range of timescales (Massey, 2005). Each element has its own story. This network of historical and contemporary interconnections forms the uniqueness of each particular place. The space of the bed in each children's book is also unique, yet it frequently shares common features with other such places. Some elements of the tableau seem fixed and permanent within the timescale of the story (often the bed itself), while for other elements, there may be a high degree of movement. In Margery Wise Brown's and Clement Hurd's *Goodnight, Moon* (1947), for instance, comparatively little movement is seen in the story, instead a series of snapshots in time is presented. Yet the composition of such scenes is complex: what stories lie behind each collection of people and artifacts? In other stories, there is substantial movement of the main character in and out of the space of the bed. *Bedtime for Frances* (1960), by Russell Hoban and Garth Williams, involves

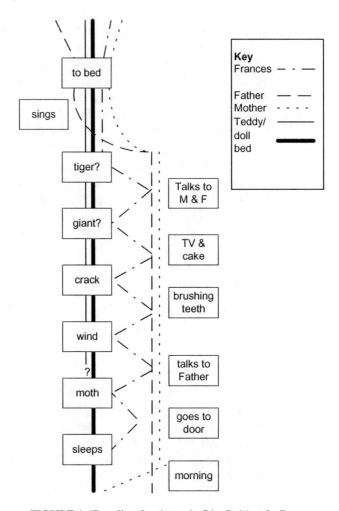

FIGURE 1 "Bundle of trajectories" in *Bedtime for Frances*.

a repetitive sequence of entrances and exits, as Frances leaves her room to tell her parents about yet another problem which is preventing her sleep (Figure 1).

Many books involve the main character taking a real or imagined journey, starting and ending at their bed, such as Maurice Sendak's *In the Night Kitchen* (1970) or John Burningham's *Oi! Get Off Our Train* (1989). This structure suggests the bed as a site of slightly boring, yet comforting, permanence—to be resisted when the protagonist is feeling adventurous, but returned to almost gratefully at the end of the story. The final location is the same, but the place is not the same because the child has changed, having gained ideas and experiences through the journeying. Occasionally, the child is asleep in the bed for almost the entire duration of the story, and instead it is other characters who carry the action, for example, toys in Alexis Deacon's *While You Are Sleeping* (2007). Even though the child may not play an active role, they are still the most important, or powerful, character in the story, to be looked after or served by those who form part of that place during the night.

Normally, adults decide on the size, shape, style, color and spatial position of a child's bed. One would assume that adult authors and illustrators make deliberate decisions about the physical appearance and positioning of beds, and thus employ them as an educational vehicle on different levels. Remarkably, children's beds in picturebooks are unimaginatively plain and boring, and often oversized. Even though the beds are almost all intended to be children's beds, it is surprising how "adult" both the frames and bedding seem to be. The overwhelming majority of frames are wooden (plain or painted) and often quite old-fashioned in design with large headboards and footboards (Figure 2). In books featuring animals rather than children, beds are unpainted wood and quite chunky, possibly reinforcing the "nature" theme, for instance Martin Waddell's and Barbara Firth's *Can't You Sleep, Little Bear?* (1988). There is also a significant minority of brass or metal bedheads, either of a Victorian style or institutional/hospital style. Very few beds are of a different design or of a different nature, such as curling up on grass.

Bedding is also often quite old-fashioned, with many instances of top-sheets, a blanket and quilt—surely quite unusual nowadays. There are a few exceptions though, in which the bedding is more modern in form and looks more like it was designed for children. Not surprisingly, all such books are from the twenty-first century. Could illustrators have been drawing on memories of sleeping at grandparents' houses? Or is there some prototype bed and bedding in Western imagination (wooden headboard and footboard, large white pillow, colored cover, or blanket with white sheet turned tidily over at the top)? Our initial argument on bed-ness rather supports the latter; yet, obviously, the adults' nostalgic reminiscences, as always in children's literature, play a prominent role.

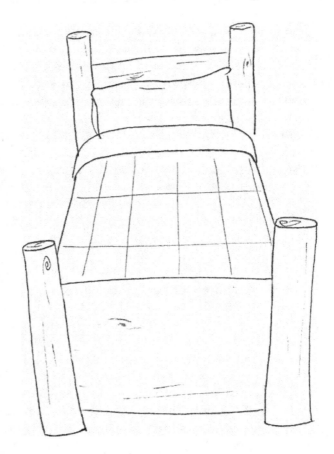

FIGURE 2 Prototype bed.

As with beds and bedding, the majority of bedrooms seem rather adult, old-fashioned and sparse for depiction of children's rooms. Among the few exceptions are *Goodnight, Moon* and *Peepo* in which bedrooms are old-fashioned but full of objects, ostensibly in order to facilitate spotting and discussion with adult. *Peace at Last* (1995) by Jill Murphy, also includes an "old-style" Mum, complete with hairnet! A dozen or so books show children's rooms (and in one case an adult room) which are believable as contemporary, with a mess on floor and a range of belongings, though some books only show limited context around the bed, so it is not possible to be precise. The form of beds and their placement in a room can reflect "oddness" in a story, for instance, isolated positioning of the bed in the middle of a field in Satoshi Kitamura's *When Sheep Cannot Sleep* (1986); rakish angles in Pija Lindenbaum's

When Owen's Mom Breathed Fire (2006); or an extremely short bed in *In the Night Kitchen*.

Transition from cradle or crib to cot to a normal bed is a significant component of a child's growth and maturation. Cradle indicates baby, cot, toddler, bed, a child. While the text of Molly Bang's counting and bedtime story *Ten, Nine, Eight* (1983) says: "big girl ready for bed," the image of the cot suggests that the parents still treat her as an infant, yet expect her to be a "big girl" who goes to bed alone and without fears. Paul's cot in *Paul Alone in the World* (1942), by Jens Sigsgaard and Arne Ungermann, also signals his young age, which does not really correspond to his subsequent self-assured actions in the empowering dreamworld. It seems that illustrators try to underscore the age of their characters by letting them sleep in a bed suitable for a considerably younger child, thus diminishing their already disempowered position.

The bed as a socialization vehicle is emphasized in many books. The protagonist of H. A. Rey's *Curious George* (1941) is brutally taken out of his normal environment in Africa where he was, according to the text, very happy, and transposed into adult and "civilized" world where he does not know the rules. "After a good meal *and a good pipe* [emphasis added], George was very tired. He crawled into bed and fell asleep at once." The little savage has to learn to eat at a table and sleep in a bed, which also includes donning sleepwear while George otherwise goes around naked. Notably, being placed in a zoo at the end of the book implies that George will return to more natural ways of sleeping.

Similarly, sleeping in a bed is a momentous part of the little elephant Babar's socialization in Jean de Brunhoff's picturebook series. Like George, Babar has to learn to eat at a table and sleep in a bed. During his honeymoon in *The Voyages of Babar* (1932), Babar is captured and treated like a beast rather than a civilized creature: "They give us straw to sleep on!" cries Babar ". . . as though we were donkeys!" The rescue is immediately confirmed by returning to proper sleeping habits: "The Old Lady lends Celeste a nightgown and provides Babar with a pair of pajamas. . . . Now they are having breakfast in bed. . ." In his elegant home, Babar has a bed appropriate to a king. The size and pattern of the bed stress the character's status.

A nursery and a separate bed is a relatively new phenomenon in the history of childhood. For centuries, children slept in shared beds, most often together with servants. In many cultures still today it is inconceivable that a young child should have a room of her own, either because of the standard of living or because of traditions. *Madeline* does not only show communal, institutional sleeping, but emphasizes conformity in the repeated "two straight lines." Yet, the archetypal Western bedtime narrative is that in which a lonely child is haunted by nightmares; besides *Bedtime for Frances*, Mercer Mayer's *There's a Nightmare in my Closet* (1968), Jan Ormerod's *Moonlight* (1982), and Nick Ward's *A Rumpus in the Night!* (2007), to name a few, spread across the time period under discussion. From the socio-historical point of view, these bedtime stories present a reflection of a contemporary, albeit conventional, image of a Western, middle-class, nuclear family, even when only one parent is explicitly portrayed. It is, however, also a symbolic reflection of the individual, unique human experience which may have little to do with any observable reality. Indeed, how can we otherwise account for the overwhelming majority of single children in a typical bedtime story? In our sample, we have just a couple of sibling narratives, only one of which features a bunk bed, *Röda hund (German Measles)*, by P.C. Jersild and Matti Lepp (1988). Anthony Brown's *The Tunnel* (1989) shows the brother sneaking into the sister's bedroom to scare her. Shared dreamscapes are highly unusual in children's books. Even in a perfectly harmonious bedtime story, such as *Goodnight, Moon*, the child is still alone; the nursery is unnaturally large and full of objects in which the figure of the adult is almost obscured. The figure—is she a grandmother or a nanny?—may create a sense of security, bur she is not even present in every picture. In one spread, the armchair is empty, in some others, it is cut off, and in the final spread the adult has left. The slightly ambiguous voice—narrator's, adult character's, child character's?—adds to the overall disturbing visual space. The Freudian interpretations view this book as a positive turning point in a child's separation process in which the child asserts his identity in his particular and personal space (Pearson, 2010). However, it is just one of possible interpretations, and Freudian ideas of childhood as inherently traumatic can be questioned. A much later picturebook, Kitty Crowther's *Alors?* (2005), might be expected to employ a more modern view of childhood, but also in this story, the child goes to bed surrounded by his toys, but without an adult to tuck him in or kiss him goodnight. One could argue that the child has in fact conquered separation anxiety by transferring it onto the toys and acting as dominant rather than dominated; yet, his seeming liberation is caused by the absence of adult affection.

A bed is, or should be, a secure place because it is familiar to all senses: the touch, the smell, the sight, the sound of creaking wood or metal. There are indeed picturebooks in which the bed is portrayed as a site of stability and comfort, such as the pleasurable bed-time reading scene in Anthony Browne's *Things I Like* (1989). There are also instances of the adult bed being a place of refuge: Michael Rosen's and Helen Oxenbury's *We're Going on a Bear Hunt* (1997) shows a comic return of four children, father and dog to the parent bed.

Yet, a child's bed can easily turn into a place of imprisonment and punishment. The visual expression of solitude and confinement is extremely gratifying. The metal bed frame in Anthony Browne's *Gorilla* (1983), separating the character from the viewer, clearly enhances the sense of captivity. The image alludes to several other images by Browne, not least caged animals. The metaphor becomes lucid in its interpictorial connection.

A child sent to bed without supper is a recurrent trope in children's fiction, even when the bed as an artifact is not featured, as in Beatrix Potter's *The Tale of Peter Rabbit* (1902). The huge intimidating bed in Sendak's *Where the Wild Things Are* (1963) dominates the room and is rather a reflection of the character's mood than a credible depiction of a material object. The visual space, stripped of all personal elements, with its gloomy, dull colors, devoid of any tokens of childhood, can hardly be perceived as a child's nursery. The disproportionally sized bed as a symbol of the child's distorted perception is a recurrent element in picturebooks. It is the central image in Dorte Karrebæk's *Den nye leger* (*The New Playmate*, 2001). The child takes refuge in her bed, which, however, does not provide consolation, but on the contrary, provokes further fears as the girl has one bizarre visitor after the other. The bed offers no comfort, and only by leaving the bed can the character escape from her grief. The bed becomes a symbol of mental disturbance.

For the little bear Mina in Anna Höglund's *Mina och Kåge* (*Mina and Kåge*, 1995), her bed becomes the place of abandonment and grief. Like so many picturebook characters, Mina's fears are conveyed through visual rather than verbal narration. The central, close up position of the bed on the page emphasizes the focus on its significance as a mental topos. The sequence of pages with Mina switching the light on and off suggests duration, iterativity, something that happens over and over again. While bedtime fear is a recurrent motif in picturebooks, it is questionable whether Mina is indeed a child. The animal disguise enables the picturebook creator to circumvent the issue of age; the two characters can be two children playing house as well as two adults living in a partnership. In the end of the book, reconciliation between the characters is manifested in their sharing a bed, which may support both interpretations; more importantly, however, is that the bed becomes a space where the characters can negotiate and reunite. While it is not uncommon to find an image of a child reconciled with parents in their bed, the sharing of space between two equal agents is unusual. As a domestic space, bed is Mina's domain; and as such she grants her playmate or partner entry much in the same manner parents would allow a child to enter their private space.

Thus, in the context of children's literature, beds frequently symbolize two radically different emotions, security or anxiety. A bed is a highly ambivalent topos, which in children's literature also acquires significance that is slightly different from general literature. Historically, the bed was considered the most important piece of furniture in the house and a status symbol. The Great Bed of Ware, displayed at the Victoria & Albert Museum in London, is a good example: a boastful display of wealth and high social position. For an adult person, a bed is a place – either a piece of furniture or a location—for sleep, relaxation and sexual activity, historically also a social place, for eating and entertaining guests. Beds are directly connected with the life cycle, including childbirth, procreation and death, which, although pertinent for the underlying levels of children's literature, are not directly manifest in it. In adults' lives, beds are ideally a shared space where affection is allowed and promoted. A child's bedroom, as represented in most picturebooks, is a lonely place, to which a child is exiled from the communal space of a living room or kitchen and confined within the strictly defined borders. The typical establishing image in a bedtime story shows a child hiding under the covers, the fingertips clutching the sheet, with the expression of fear in the face (Figure 3). Alternatively, the child is depicted sitting up in bed, crying. Toys are at best the only companions in a child's bed. An imaginary friend, such as the eponymous character in John

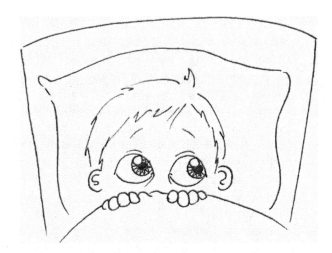

FIGURE 3 Common representation of bedtime fear.

Burningham's *Aldo* (1991), can play a similar role. Parents' bedrooms are normally out of bounds for children, and the invasion
of this adult space is a serious offence, only allowed through the
playfulness of carnival. In Dr. Seuss's *The Cat in the Hat* (1957), for
instance, the general chaos created by the naughty visitor finally
reaches the parents' bedroom. The vivacious protagonist of *The
Wild Baby* (1981), by Barbro Lindgren and Eva Eriksson, intrudes
into mother's bedroom just as he previously conquers the kitchen
and the living room, firmly stating his right to be everywhere. Yet,
a harmonious relationship between the child and the adult can
be emphasized exactly by the permission to enter the adult space,
as seen in many images from Sven Nordqvist's *Festus and Mercury*
series, where Mercury the mischievous cat is allowed to play in bed
with his foster father. Moreover, an adult can be invited to share
the child's bed in a similarly carnivalesque manner, as in the image
in Pija Lindenbaum's *Else-Marie and Her Seven Daddies* (1991),
where the miniature daddies—obviously imaginary, although the
verbal text never says so—cuddle in the girl's bed while she is reading a book for them. Such reversal of conditions is unusual, but it
emphasizes adult normativity, in which it is the adult who decides
how the privacy of the bed is to be employed.

A bed is often the only private space that a child has, the only
refuge, but it can be unquestionably intruded into by adults, sometimes quite violently, as in Dorte Karrebæk's *Pigen der var go til*

mange ting (*The Girl who was Good at Many Things*, 1996), where visual framing and framebreaking becomes an efficient device to convey the child's total vulnerability: adults literally invade the child's private space, as images leak into it from their own. This is a highly unusual book in its ruthless portrayal of adulthood. Yet, even in considerably less radical stories, adults' supremacy is prevalent. The adults decide when the child is to go to bed and when to get up. *Oi! Get Off Our Train* starts with the mother saying: "Get to bed immediately. You know you have to be up early for school tomorrow," and ends in: "You must get up immediately, or you will be late for school." The bedside seems to be the only space where the child and the parent interact, yet not for comfort, but for conflict. Likewise, Satoshi Kitamura's *Me and My Cat* (1999) starts by: "Nicholas, wake up! You will be late for school". The child's feelings are seldom addressed; in Lindenbaum's *Else-Marie and her Seven Daddies* the protagonist-narrator states:

> It feels like this is just the morning when I'd like to sleep in. Just a little while!
> —Get up now, Mum cries and opens the window. But under the blanket it is warm and dark. If I didn't have to go, I'd pretend to be still asleep.

The role of parents in all these books is more than dubious; yet, as in all children's literature, it is a subjective view, the child's image of the dictatorial parent. It is only occasionally that the roles can be reversed, once again in a carnevalesque mode. In Lindenbaum's *When Owen's Mom Breathed Fire* the boy has to wake his mother up when she is depressed, which is metaphorically depicted through her transforming into a dragon. In the image, she is hiding under the covers, reluctant to get up and face another day of problems. Interestingly enough, the child is portrayed as more mature than the adult; he is gentle and considerate, taking his mother through the day even though he does not quite understand what is going on. More commonly, a child who is sent to bed cannot attract his mother's attention even by turning into a monster, as does the protagonist of David McKee's *Not Now, Bernard* (1980).

The bed as a battlefield for child/parent power manifestations is featured in dozens of picturebooks. The issues of power are enacted between adults and children as well as between children and fantasy images to which they ascribe power through fear, for instance, monsters under beds. Three patterns emerge quite clearly in these power negotiations: subjugation, transgression and subversion. The subjugation, when children are dominated and put in their "place" (bed) by adult, ranges in intensity from gentle persuasion and understanding in *Can't You Sleep Little Bear* to verbal and physical domination overstated to the level of humor. Many of these bedtime-conflict stories, characteristically entitled *I Don't Want to Go to Bed* or *I Can't Sleep,* play out the trivial scenario in which the child is trying to resist the inevitable triumph of the parents through delaying and attention-seeking tactics: first by demanding water, then claiming that there are monsters in the closet or under the bed. Tony Ross's *I Don't Want to Go to Bed* (2003) voices the adult supremacy by the categorical: "Bed is good for you." This book, like many others, also contains a strong didactic message as after the nightly battle the child is too tired in the morning. Astrid Lindgren's and Ilon Wikland's *I Don't Want to Go to Bed* (1988) shows the child who, after watching through magical eye-glasses the many small animals getting tucked down and hugged by their parents, realizes that bed and sleep are indeed good for him. The typical outcome of a bedtime story, "and at last, the child was asleep," signals the adults' victory.

The bedtime situation provides a starting point for nightmares, yet in most books the motif of fear is reversed, in an estranging, cathartic effect. In the tame and light-hearted stories with stereotypical titles such as *Under the Bed, What's Under the Bed, Don't Look Under the Bed!, The Monster Under the Bed, Monsters Under the Bed!, There's a Monster Under my Bed, There is an Octopus Under my Bed, There's an Alligator Under My Bed,* and so on, the monsters are seldom visualized, and the reader is supposed to feel superior to the protagonists, laughing at their ungrounded fears.[1] As often in children's literature, transgression becomes a pedagogical device, for instance, in terms of activities not normally allowed in own bed space (kangaroos jumping on bed in *One Bear at Bedtime*); or in another's bed space (a child standing on adult's bed to express disapproval in *Her Majesty, Aunt Essie*); or threats of

---

[1] Interestingly enough, there are a vast number of books on parenting and an occasional book on management entitled *Monsters under the Bed*.

others to transgress on own familiar bed space, which need resisting. Most monster-under-bed books aim to dispel children's fears by exploring power reversals. Fears can be given a concrete shape, most typically a huge, hairy creature, as in *There's a Nightmare in my Closet*; yet the child is empowered since the monster is more scared than the child. There are many variations on this popular, highly didactic theme, in which the creatures under the bed are frightened by the child. In Paul Bright and Ben Cort's *Under the Bed* (2003), for instance, direct address, "the frightening thing in the bed is YOU!", reverses the direction of fear, also involving the reader. Alternatively, as in *A Rumpus a Night!* (2007) the child and the monster are equally afraid of each other, but become friends. In this book, parallel images featuring the child and the monster emphasize the mirroring of emotions and perpetual reversal of power. In *One Bear at Bedtime*, a child successfully manages the invasion of monsters with his teddy as a guardian. Resistance to fears is encouraged; for example, in Gene Kemp's and Diann Timms's *Matty's Midnight Monster* (1991), the monster gains power and size as the protagonist fears him, but then shrinks and is disempowered to a slightly pathetic figure by her resistance. Yet, even though all these books have a humorous flavor, the bed is still a lonely place for protagonists, a place of regular nightly exile where they have to learn, each in their own way, to cope with the frightening experience.

The bed can further be more ambivalent. In Neil Gaiman's and Dave McKean's *The Wolves in the Walls* (2003), the bed creates a false sense of security, since the child is exposed to fears and anxieties exactly because she is left alone in bed. The images convey a direct sense of threat, where words may not be sufficient. The hesitation as to the reality of the events is emphasized by the contradiction of words and images. Sleep in itself is an ambivalent state, in between life and death, a situation when one completely loses control, and dreams and nightmares bring forward our deepest and most secret emotions. In Stefan Mählqvist's and Tord Nygren's *Come into My Night, Come into My Dream* (1978), the title prompts an interpretation, while images, rife with interpictorial allusions, clearly show how the child's nightmares are induced by the adults' neglect. The trajectory, in Massey's (2005) terms, of the protagonist leads him from his bed through an array of nightmares to his parents' bed where he practically returns to the womb by taking off his clothes and curling up in fetal position between his parents. Rather than developing an independent identity, the child regresses to a pre-individual state. This explicitly retrograde movement is unusual in picturebooks and in children's literature in general; but it can be argued whether narratives featuring beds as a starting and ending place demonstrate stability, even if that stability is initially resented, as in *Where the Wild Things Are*. The closure can be viewed as the resistance to adults resolved by the end of the story, and the child has doubtless employed his imagination through escaping temporarily into a fantastic space of his own, but the mother is still absent on his return, and she has power to grant or deny him food.

Conversely, beds can become highly creative spaces allowing a carnivalesque transformation of fear and anxiety into fun and adventure. One of such relatively rare books is Burningham's *Oi! Get Off Our Train!,* which efficiently subverts adult authority. The mother's firmly pointed finger, ordering the child to bed, is an exercise of power and an intrusion into the child's private space of play. Further, by her contempt for the child's transition object, the pajama-case dog, the mother expresses her discontent with the child's immature attachment. The child seemingly obliges, following the mother's order "Now settle down and go to sleep"; the image shows him with his eyes shut. Maybe he is pretending. The next image zooms on the bed, making it occupy the whole panel of the page, thus foregrounding both the material object and the idea of peaceful sleep. The adventure begins, the child has full control, and eventually his imagination will triumph over the mother's mental abuse. There are no images suggesting that the child is scared or unhappy, and the closure is indeed a movement far beyond the initial situation. Similarly, Sendak's *In the Night Kitchen* opens with the image of fear going over to irritation going over to rage. Rather than succumbing to fears, the child channels them through nonsensical play where images, not unexpectedly, acquire the leading role. The contrast between the opening and closing images emphasizes the child's successful conquest of anxieties. Typically for Sendak, the adults are conspicuously absent from the narrative, the bakers being merely grotesque correspondences to the wild things in Max's mindscape in *Where the Wild Things Are*. The difference between Sendak's two books is that the bedtime frame is more explicit in *In the*

Night Kitchen, and the word "night" in the title further accentuates this aspect.

It can be rewarding to compare two books with similar transformation plots, Satoshi Kitamura's *Me and my Cat* and David Almond's and Stephen Lambert's *Kate, the Cat and the Moon* (2004). In both, the child resists adult power through compensatory fantasy. The nearly exact repetition of two images in Kitamura's book, in the beginning and end of the narrative, suggests that the day when Nicholas has turned into a cat only takes place in the instant while mother is dragging him out of bed, in a true act of violence. (Let us remember, however, that it is the child subjective view of the mother's actions). To justify his wild imagination, the protagonist provides an explanation, the figure of a witch—incidentally, placed before the title page and thus easy to overlook—transferring his own responsibility onto an adult still more powerful than the mother. The second book shows a different kind of imaginative metamorphosis, ostensibly a typically feminine one. The tomcat that Nicholas is transformed into represents the boy's lust for freedom and adventure; the plot is humorous and carnivalesque. When Kate becomes a cat, it reflects the mystical, nocturnal nature of cats and their traditional connection with female witchcraft. It is never mentioned that Kate is afraid of the dark, and the family is presented as friendly and harmonious, yet the child definitely uses the liminal space of the bed for powerful imaginative play.

Still more subversive is the employment of beds for magical transportation, either for floating, as in Stefan Mählqvist's and Tord Nygren's *I'll Take Care of the Crocodiles* (1978) or flying, as in Svein Nyhus' *Jeg!* (*I!*, 2004). The portmanteau image of bedbook in Remy Charlip's and Jon J. Muth's *Why I Will Never Ever Ever Ever Have Enough Time to Read This Book* (2000) is playful in itself, drawing the viewer's attention to the metafictional nature of the narrative. Like many bedtime narratives, the story is framed by the nearly identical images of the child asleep in bed, yet the story does not involve a dream, but daytime packed with small, insignificant events. This very reversal of the conventional bedtime story becomes subversive.

Some of the plots, not least the dream and metamorphosis plots, can also appear in children's novels; Mary Norton's *Bedknob and Broomstick* (1947) is an obvious example. However, it is the visual, material world of the picturebook that allows the strong literal focus on the bed as a significant childhood space. Through considering in depth the material form of the bed as reflected in the visual narratives of picturebooks, we could more easily understand the various functions of the objects; the issues of power negotiations connected with them; and the role of beds as a meeting place, in Massey's (2005) sense. After all, young children spent nearly half of their time in bed.

References

Galbraight, Mary. "'Goodnight Nobody' Revisited: Using an Attachment Perspective to Study Picture Books about Bedtime." *Children's Literature Association Quarterly* 23.4 (1998-99): 172–80. Print.

Goga, Nina. Bedtime for democracy. Soverommet i nyere norske bildebøker. *Barnebokkritikk.no.* Web. Accessed 22 Aug 2010. <http://www.barnebokkritikk.no/modules.php?name=News&file=article&sid=20>

Massey, Doreen B. *For Space.* London: Sage, 2005. Print.

Moebius, William. "Room with a View: Bedroom Scenes in Picture Books." *Children's Literature* 19 (1991): 53–74. Print.

Pearson, Claudia. *Have a Carrot: Oedipal Theory and Symbolism in Margaret Wise Brown's Bunny Trilogy.* Look Again Press, 2010. Web. <http://www.smashwords.com/books/view/21324>

Peirce, C. S. "On the Nature of Signs." *Peirce on Signs: Writings on Semiotic.* Ed. James Hoopes. Chapel Hill, NC: University of North Carolina Press, 1994. 141–43. Print.

Spitz, Ellen Handler. *Inside Picture Books.* New Haven: Yale University Press, 1999. Print.

Tatar, Maria. *The Enchanted Hunters.* New York: Norton, 2009. Print.

Children's Books Cited and Consulted

Ahlberg, Janet, and Allan Ahlberg. *Peepo!* London: Viking, 1981. Print.

Almond, David, and Stephen Lambert. *Kate, the Cat and the Moon.* London: Hodder, 2004. Print.

Apperley, Dawn. *There is an Octopus Under my Bed.* London: Bloomsbury, 2001. Print.

Armitage, Ronda and David. *One Moonlit Night.* London: Deutch, 1983. Print.

Bang, Molly. *Ten, Nine, Eight.* New York: Greenwillow, 1983. Print.

Beckman, Kaj, and Per Beckman. *Lisa Cannot Sleep.* London: Franklin Watts, 1970. Print.

Bemelmans, Ludwig. *Madeline.* New York: Putnam, 1939. Print.

Bergman, Mara and Nick Maland. *Oliver Who Would Not Sleep*. London: Hodder, 2007. Print.

Bergström, Gunilla. *Is There a Monster, Alfie Atkins*. New York: Farrar/R & S, 1988. Print.

Bright, Paul, and Ben Cort, *Under the Bed*. London: Little Tiger Press, 2003. Print.

Brown, Margaret Wise, and Clement Hurd. *Goodnight, Moon*. New York: Harper & Row, 1947. Print.

Browne, Anthony. *Gorilla*. London: Julia MacRae Books, 1983. Print.

—. *The Tunnel*. London: Julia MacRae Books, 1989. Print.

—. *Things I Like*. London: Walker Books, 1989. Print.

Burningham, John. *Aldo*. London: Jonathan Cape, 1991. Print.

—. *The Magic Bed*. London: Jonathan Cape, 2003. Print.

—. *Oi! Get Off Our Train*. London: Jonathan Cape, 1989. Print.

Charlip, Remy, and Jon J. Muth. *Why I Will Never Ever Ever Ever Have Enough Time to Read This Book*. New York: Tricycle Press, 2000. Print.

Child, Lauren. *Who's Afraid of the Big Bad Book?* London: Hodder, 2008. Print.

Collington, Peter. *On Christmas Eve*. London: Heinemann, 1990. Print.

Crowther, Kitty. *Alors?* Paris: L'école des loisirs, 2005. Print.

Dahle, Gro, and Svein Nyhus. *Roy*. Oslo: Cappelen Damm, 2008. Print.

Deacon, Alexis. *While You are Sleeping*. London: Random House, 2006. Print.

De Brunhoff, Jean. *Bonjour, Babar!* New York: Random House, 2000. Print.

Dupasquier, Philippe. *I Can't Sleep*. London: Walker Books, 1989. Print.

Dyer, Kevin. *The Monster under the Bed*. Aurora Metro, 2009. Print.

Ekman, Fam. *Kattens skrekk*. Oslo: Cappelen, 1992. Print.

Fenton, Joe. *What's Under the Bed?* New York: Simon & Schuster, 2008. Print.

Foreman, Michael. *Dad! I Can't Sleep*. London: Andersen Press, 1994. Print.

Gaiman, Neil and Dave McKean. *The Wolves in the Walls*. London: Bloomsbury, 2003. Print.

Glitz, Angelica, and Imke Sonnichsen. *Don't Look Under the Bed!* Franklin Watts, 2001. Print.

Hoban, Russell, and Garth Williams. *Bedtime for Frances*. New York: Harper, 1960. Print.

Höglund, Anna. *Mina och Kåge*. Stockholm: Alfabeta, 1995. Print.

Howe, James, and David Rose. *There is a Monster Under My Bed*. New York: Atheneum, 1990. Print.

Inkpen, Mick. *One Bear at Bedtime*. London: Hodder, 1987. Print.

Jersild, P. C. and Matti Lepp. *Röda hund*. Stockholm: Carlsen/if, 1988. Print.

Karrebæk, Dorte. *Pigen der var go til mange ting*, Copenhagen: Forum, 1996. Print.

—. *Den nye leger*. Copenhagen: Gyldendal, 2001. Print.

Kemp, Gene, and Diann Timms. *Matty's Midnight Monster*. London: Faber, 1991. Print.

Kitamura, Satoshi. *Me and My Cat*. London: Andersen Press, 1999. Print.

—. *When Sheep Cannot Sleep: The Counting Book*. London: Random House, 1986. Print.

Leonard Hill, Susan, and Mike Wohnoutka. *Can't Sleep without Sheep*. London: Bloomsbury, 2011. Print.

Lindenbaum, Pija. *Else-Marie and Her Seven Daddies*. New York: Holt, 1991. Print.

—. *When Owen's Mom Breathed Fire*. Stockholm: R&S, 2006. Print.

Lindgren, Astrid, and Ilon Wikland. *I Don't Want to Go to Bed*. New York: Farrar/R & S, 1988. Print.

Lindgren, Barbro, and Eva Eriksson. *The Wild Baby*. New York: Greenwillow, 1981. Print.

Mählqvist, Stefan and Tord Nygren. *Come into my Night, Come into my Dream*. London: Pepper Press, 1981.

—. *I'll Take Care of the Crocodiles*. New York: Atheneum, 1978. Print.

Manning, Mick, and Brita Granstrom. *What's Under the Bed*. Franklin Watts, 1997. Print.

Mayer, Mercer. *There's a Nightmare in My Closet*. New York: Dial Books, 1968. Print.

—. *There's an Alligator Under My Bed*. New York: Macmillan, 1988. Print.

McKee, David. *Not Now, Bernard*. London: Andersen Press, 1980. Print.

Murphy, Jill. *Peace at Last*. London: Macmillan, 1980. Print.

Nordqvist, Sven. *When Findus Was Little and Disappeared*. New York: Hawthorn, 2008. Print.

Norton, Mary. *Bedknob and Broomstick* (1945, 1947). Harmondsworth, Penguin, 1981. Print.

Nyhus, Svein. *Jeg!* Oslo: Gyldendal, 2004. Print.

Ormerod, Jan. *Moonlight*. London: Lothrop, 1982. Print.

Park, Barbara. *Junie B. Jones Has a Monster under her Bed*. New York: Random House, 2004.

Potter, Beatrix. *The Tale of Peter Rabbit*. London: Warne, 1902. Print.

Rey, H. A. *Curious George*. Boston: Houghton Mifflin, 1941. Print.

Rosen, Michael, and Helen Oxenbury. *We're Going on a Bear Hunt*. London: Walker Books, 1997. Print.

Ross, Tony. *I Don't Want to Go to Bed*. London: Andersen Press, 2003. Print.

Schwartz, Amy. *Her Majesty, Aunt Essie*. New York: Bradbury, 1984. Print.

Sendak, Maurice. *In the Night Kitchen*. New York: Harper, 1970. Print.

—. *The Sign on Rosie's Door*. New York: Harper, 1969. Print.

—. *Where the Wild Things Are*. New York: Harper, 1963. Print.

Seuss, Dr. *The Cat in the Hat*. New York: Random House, 1957. Print.

Sigsgaard, Jens, and Arne Ungermann. *Paul Alone in the World*. St Louis: McGraw-Hill, 1964. Print.

Stephenson, Anne M. *The Monster under the Bed*. Trafford, 2005. Print.

Sykes, Julie, and Tim Warnes. *I Don't Want to Go to Bed!* Little Tiger Press, 1997. Print.

Tan, Shaun. *The Red Tree*. Port Melbourn, Lothian, 2000. Print.

Waddell, Martin, and Barbara Firth. *Can't You Sleep, Little Bear?* London: Walker Books, 1988. Print.

Ward, Nick. *A Rumpus in the Night!* Meadowside, 2007. Print.

Watterson, Bill. *Something Under the Bed is Drooling: A Calvin and Hobbes Collection*. New York: Sphere, 1989. Print.

PICTUREBOOKS AND MULTIPLE READINGS: *WHEN WE LIVED IN UNCLE'S HAT* BY PETER STAMM AND JUTTA BAUER

JEAN WEBB

Institute of Humanities and Creative Arts, University of Worcester,
Worcester, UK

The award winning picturebook When We Lived in Uncle's Hat *by Peter Stamm and Jutta Bauer, was originally published in German in 2005 and translated into English in 2006. It is a surreal picturebook that moves the child subject from place to place where the family temporarily lives. Many of these eighteen locations are surreal places such as "In Uncle's Hat." This chapter will discuss the possible readings of this text: from that of the "proposed" reading suggested by the publishers in their support for teachers' activities with children; from the differences in a reading which uses the original cover in German that depicted children in a play situation; and, finally, from that of an existentialist philosophical perspective combined with the surreal mode of the text.*

When We Lived in Uncle's Hat is an award winning picturebook by Peter Stamm and Jutta Bauer; it was originally published in German in 2005 and translated into English in 2006. Peter Stamm, the author, is Swiss and the illustrator, Jutta Bauer, is German and lives in the city of Hamburg. Jutta Bauer is a celebrated author and illustrator in Germany and won the Hans Christian Andersen award in 2010; however, in addition to *When We Lived in Uncle's Hat,* only two of her books have been translated into English: *Selma* (2007) by Gecko, a New Zealand Press, and *Grandpa's Angels* by Walker Books (2005), which is now out of print.

The reason why I have chosen this text, in addition to it being an interesting and unusual work for the British market, is that it opens areas of discussion around the multiplicity of readings that are available through picturebooks. In addition, as it is translated from German, questions can be raised about transference from one culture to another and the implications for the reading experience. My approaches to the readings of this text are in relation to the implications of changes made to the cover when produced for the English market; additions to the title when marketed by Amazon; the notes for teachers provided by the publisher, Winged Chariot Press; interpretation given by the publicity surrounding the Tutti Frutti Leeds based theatre company's adaption of *When We Lived in Uncle's Hat*; and, finally, my personal interpretation as an adult reader.

First a brief description of the picturebook will help to frame the discussion. *When We Lived in Uncle's Hat* is a surreal work where family and the child subject move from place to place to temporary and very unusual accommodations. There are eighteen locations. I have included the full list here to emphasize the imaginative and surreal nature of these locations:

1. The house with the blue light
2. The bus
3. The forest
4. The church roof
5. Aunty's violin
6. The hotel
7. Nowhere
8. The house with three phones
9. The moon
10. The cinema
11. The rain
12. The white tent in the snow
13. The sea
14. Uncle's hat
15. On my own
16. A different bridge every night
17. The dream
18. Our house

Although the illustrations have not been included here for copyright reasons, both text and illustration as extracted pages can be viewed on the Winged Chariot Press website (http://www.wingedchariot.com/docs/Uncle'sHat%20support.pdf).

The book is constructed with no center page spread; instead each location is contained within two facing pages: there is text on one side with a black and white strip illustration at the bottom of that page depicting the family members moving and opposite a full color, full page illustration. The illustrations have more in them than the text describes.

The locations seem to be randomly selected; however, this reflects the surreal nature of the work which partially applies to the structure as well as the content. In each location there are references to what they do there and to other members of the family. For example in the section where they reside on the bus:

> When we lived on the bus we paid no rent, but we had to punch a new ticket every hour. We met lots of people, but they all looked so serious and were always too busy to talk. Sometimes we hid under the seats and listened to the engine roaring like a lion. Sometimes we'd press the "stop" button, even though we didn't want to get off. The whole day smelt of petrol and sweat and we saw the same streets over and over again. We could only read at the railways station when the bus stopped for a few minutes to wait for the trains or simply for the hands of the clock to move.
>
> Mother learnt four languages.
> Grandpa lost three teeth.
> My brother made two new friends and Grandma got pneumonia.
> But Father fell out with Mother.
> So. . . . we moved to the forest. (6)

The text follows a similar pattern throughout the book. The reader engages with the text; drops down to the black and white strip at the bottom of the page; moves to the pictures and then, in my own reading habit with this book, returns to the illustration of the family moving onward. Throughout the book, the reading requires consideration of the relationship between the elements of the text and how these change as one moves through the reading experience both within the particular location and the book as a whole. The "story" of the family is told in fragments, with snippets of information given about various family members, as in the aforementioned example.

The original cover of the book in the German depicts children playing beneath a table, which was, from my experiences as a mother with young children at playgroup and as a teacher, in addition to my own childhood remembrances, a favorite and simple way of playing "house." In the English version, the illustration of the episode "When We Lived in Uncles Hat" is repeated as the cover. The hat is tipped as Uncle inclines his head and the various members of the family are somewhat precariously placed. Grandmother is washing dishes at a sink and a tea cup and saucer are slipping off the brim destined to smash on the ground below from the height of Uncle. The parents are set racing on a divan bed with the angle of the brim, their hair swept back and their mouths open as if on a helter-skelter. The cat, fur on end and mouth agape, one supposes in a yowl, is on the bridge of Uncle's nose. In short, this is a precarious place to live, on the edge, the brim of disaster. The shift to this illustration made by the English publishers accentuates the surreal and unusual tone of the work. One wonders if this is a family of miniature people like Mary Norton's The Borrowers, or whether they are life sized in a land of giants, or perhaps bewitched by an "Uncle" who has captured them for his own, perhaps unsavory, ends. The shift takes the scene away from the direct possibilities of thinking that the work is a set of imaginings by a group of children, into a set of imaginings by the author and artist and the narrator. I am not suggesting, nor arguing, that one illustration would be better or more suitable, but that by changing the cover the set of possibilities has changed, and I think become more serious, as I will develop later in my personal reading of this thought-provoking and outstanding picturebook.

The change made to the title by the marketing people on the current English version, still published by Winged Chariot Press, has the title *When We Lived in Uncle's Hat and Other Incredible Places*. My version purchased when it first came on to the English market does not have the subtitle. The addition changes the expectations of the reader somewhat. Without it you read through the book in a constant state of surprise and wonderment, trying to work out what the connections might be between places, what the particular places mean, and moreover, why were those situations chosen. The subtitle takes away a little of the unexpectedness since the expectation becomes that these will be "incredible" places to live, and that is perhaps is the point of the work.

The notes for teachers produced by Winged Chariot Press under the heading "Using Stories From Winged Chariot Press" states that they have selected *When We Lived in Uncle's Hat* to: "offer children an excellent transition between typical picturebooks and their first 'chapter' books." (http://www.wingedchariot.com/docs/Uncle'sHat/support.pdf).

This is an admirable intention; however, I would challenge how useful this text would be for young readers if this is the primary intention for selection, which is suggested as it is their first statement about the book. The notion of chapters can be applied in a simplistic way in that each time the page is turned a new place is entered, yet the way that the settings and the situations are interconnected is far more subtle. I would suggest that they are more subtle and more demanding than conventional interlinked chapters in a text. Here the reader has so much more to do than being directed by a narrator. This is a postmodern work where the gaps for the reader to fill in are frequent and ever open; where the essential emotions of life are confronted and explored and also evaded. The approaches suggested are, to me, reductive and do not do justice to this rich and moving work of art and literature. There is far more which could be done than principally asking children to imagine living in unusual places in a rather mundane fashion "discussing homelessness" and identifying the nouns. Yet to do justice to the publishers they have brought to the reader of English a rich and stimulating work, which cannot be under estimated in a publishing market where translation is so rare. *When We Lived in Uncle's Hat* is a moving puzzle of experiences both physically and emotionally as the reader journeys through a life which may encounter real places, or may be the imaginative mind of a child trying to find an emotional equation in a manifestation of place for their inner, otherwise silenced feelings.

The publicity for the adaption of *When We Lived in Uncle's Hat* as a play by the Tutti Frutti Company runs as follows:

This is a play about . . . how walls don't make a house,
And doors don't make a house.
It's a play about how a family makes a house. And it doesn't matter where you live—whether it's an up house or a down house, or an outhouse or a townhouse—who you live with is the important bit. (Tutti Frutti Company)

It suggests that the dramatic adaptation, which I regret not to have seen as yet, does focus on the surreal interpretation of place and the familial relationships which are paramount. The portrayal of the surreality of the work is outstanding in relation to books currently available from the majority of British publishing houses. Picturebooks published by Italian and French houses, for example, are far more cutting edge and risk taking in terms of imagination and creativity than a good deal of the work normally available in English. This becomes a tricky area of discussion, since I have seen work by British artists that is highly challenging (in a positive sense, as is this text) and imaginative, and of the highest artistic and imaginative quality, yet would be hard pressed to find a UK publisher, in what is principally a conservative market. There are several British artists who have been successfully published in this mode of work and they are rightly internationally celebrated; however, it is not my intention to turn this discussion of the text into a polemical argument about the UK publishing industry.

The reason why I elected to talk about this book is because it engendered in me a sense of dislocation and a considerable depth of feeling which would not be apparent from the currently available publicity. The questions which arose from my reading of this picturebook were about stability, location, familial relationships, reality, and subjectivity. The movement from place to place reflects the incessant movement of the family. The final place is "Our house" where there is a sense of the child subject having found a place of peace and rest. The starting place is the "House with the Blue Light." I asked some German friends if there was any significance in the choice of the blue light. Apparently, as in the United Kingdom, it is associated with a police station, which did not pick up on any particular resonances in this way. This seems to be a time without rest for the family and the pervasive impression throughout the book from this initial introduction:

> Father read four newspapers, Mother bought three chairs.
> Grandma knitted two pairs of striped socks for each of us and Grandpa lost his sunglasses.
> But my sister was always sad. So . . . we moved to the bus. (5)

The illustration is one which could be readily placed in contemporary German city life. However, this is also through my association with having regularly spent time in Munich, and I "read" contemporary urban/domestic German architecture in the pictures. The three-story house is in a square and the figures are silhouetted as the viewer looks down upon the scene from a height. The reader is an observant viewer, seeing the outlines of the familial figures against the lighted windows. The sign of a Dance Hall runs down the side of the building and the cat is picked out sitting in the blue lighted entrance way. The blue light suggests wakefulness, as blue light is used for "wake up" alarms on modern clocks. The over-riding pervasiveness of this picture is that of being alone, a looker on, watching life from a distance. The narrator is inside the family and yet by positioning the narrator also as "the artist," since the narrator is presenting these places to the reader, the insider is also "outside." The sense of distance is increased for the English reader since the German-ness of the illustrations has been retained. In places, as "On the Bus," the German advertising captions and graffiti have not been translated into English, adding to an unfamiliarity within an otherwise familiar scene. This is a most refreshing approach by the publishers. Over the past twenty years since I have been talking in my professional capacity with picturebook illustrators and authors, I have often heard that work in translation has to be "massaged" to fit the recipient culture, or else publishers think that it will fail to sell because it will not be readily understandable to an American or English readership. Here, the understated German characteristics add just another distancing from English reality: similar, but not the same.

To me this text goes further than being "surreal," which more readily describes some of the locations demonstrating that in life which cannot be readily described in terms of normal physicality. Stamm and Bauer have in this work actually and philosophically moved into the realms of existentialism. The text moves beyond the boundaries of "normal" existence yet it is also located within a familial network of relationships. The child subject here has no control over where he/she is living, except for when they elect to move out on their own. The emphasis falls on location and requires the reader to consider the nature of the location and the related experiences, that is, how the family exists. Considering the existentialist nature of the work was helpful in trying to make a kind of "sense" of the text, for:

> Existentialism is centered upon the analysis of existence and of the way humans find themselves existing in the world. The notion is that humans exist first and then each individual spends a lifetime changing their essence or nature.

Furthermore:

> through free will, choice, and personal responsibility. The belief is that people are searching to find out who and what they are throughout life as they make choices based on their experiences, beliefs, and outlook. And personal choices become unique without the necessity of an objective form of truth. An existentialist believes that a person should be forced to choose and be responsible without the help of laws, ethnic rules, or traditions. ("Existentialism")

The positioning of the child subject is moderated as there are limitations on the freedom of the child per se, which are explored when he/she decides to move into living alone. Consideration of some of the statements made by André Breton in the *Manifesto of Surrealism* (1924) was also enlightening. Breton reflects on the adult state as follows:

> If he still retains a certain lucidity, all he can do is turn back toward his childhood which, however his guides and mentors may have botched it, still strikes him as somehow charming. There, the absence of any known restrictions allows him the perspective of several lives lived at once; this illusion becomes firmly rooted within him; now he is only interested in the fleeting, the extreme facility of everything. Children set off each day without a worry in the world. Everything is near at hand, the worst material conditions are fine. The woods are white or black. . . .

Breton continued with his thoughts on the imagination as follows:

> This imagination, which knows no bounds, is henceforth allowed to be exercised only in strict accordance with the laws of an arbitrary utility. (Breton)

Thus, the combination of existentialism and surrealism combined to provide a philosophical framework for the reading of this text. It also raised a number of personal considerations about my own approach to life. To explain, Breton continued in the Manifesto to comment on the restrictions and inefficacy of rationality. Yet, from my own perspective, I know that I need to find some way of "making sense" of rationalizing what I learned and experienced from this reading. I identified the constants which are employed throughout the book: the layout and suggested reading pattern as previously described. Furthermore, in the prose sections there are repeated patterns. There is a description of the lived experience within the particular location that relates to those circumstances. For example, when the family lived on the moon:

> It was quiet especially at night. In the evening the earth rose and in the morning it set. . . . We were surrounded by seas, but we could not swim in any of them. (20)

Following the prose section, there is always a short section of five or six lines which is a reflection on the circumstances of various family members. Reading across these accounts one pieces together an ongoing account of the family. One learns that Grandma is an important figure, as is Grandpa. Grandma is generally busy and a provider in her way by knitting socks. Grandpa undergoes a gradual deterioration from losing three teeth on the bus; to becoming forgetful when they live "Nowhere"; feeling sad on the church roof when he observes each time someone is buried; and, then, to his own death under the three bridges. It also becomes evident that the relationship between the Mother and Father is strained. "On the bus" Father falls out with Mother; in "Nowhere" he is "very bored"; in the "House With Three Phones" he lives on the fourth floor, yet there are only three phones, implying that he may not have joined in the storytelling via phone in which the children engage. These short sections give a cameo of living within this family; of the loves, losses, the quirky behavior, and the circumstances of their relationships. For instance, when they are in "The Dream" the Mother does not recognize the child any more. The pattern of inclusion is not repeated throughout, the Grandparents and parents appear frequently and the other siblings occasionally. When they live "In Uncle's Hat," the section focuses upon him, observing his life, as it were, from the brim, from the perspective of an adult who is so strained and perhaps depressed that he is losing his grip on what seems to be a rather loveless life:

> There were four times when Uncle said nothing at all.
> Three times he forgot something important and couldn't remember it.
> He met two women on a regular basis but kissed only one of them.
> But his hat gave him a headache. (30)

These codas having a repeated patterning within them based on the figures four, three, and two. In each circumstance there is an observation, which in some way includes this sequence of numbers, but is innovatively adapted to the circumstance. "On The Moon," for example:

> Grandma said everything on the moon was only a quarter of its normal weight.
> Father promised us each a third of the world.
> Mother slept half the time . . . (20)

The following line of this kind of verse contains a personal comment, as when on the moon:

> . . . Grandpa missed his girlfriends and his best mate . . .

What begins as a scientific observation passing on such facts to the children and child reader becomes an observation and insight into the feelings and hopes of the adult world that can never be realized. There is a recurrent element of sadness as with the Uncle himself.

The final line always begins: "So . . ." (with a slight pause indicated) and then where they are to move to next. The inclusion of the mathematical pattern gives both a rhythm and a kind of constancy. It is somewhat like counting stairs as you mount them, the kind of ritual behavior associated with an obsessive compulsive syndrome. The pattern is a constant which gives a sense of security and comfort, as are the red rug and the cat which mostly appear throughout.

The pictures themselves are frames as though taken from an exercise book, thus giving the impression of a visual journal through the family's travels. Very often the pictures depict a lack of communication, the gaze of the subjects do not meet, as typified by the final frame in "Our House." Yet, there are also images of a close family unit as in "Nowhere" when they are clustered closely together sitting looking upward; the youngest child is asleep nestled up to his father while Grandpa sits attached, yet detached, positioned behind them and looking the other way into his own space. Extra pieces of information are also included which provide amusing and also poignant cameos. "On the Church Roof," for example, mother sunbathes nude on the church dome while one child directs waste water poured through a gargoyle in the direction of the pastor who stands below remonstrating. His action can be read as paradoxical, since traditionally the church has been a place of sanctuary, but perhaps not if one is to occupy the roof. Meanwhile, father sits at a table, his head resting upon his hand in a sad and distracted manner, a glass of wine at his elbow. Text and image work together to tell the family stories both verbally and silently. The reader becomes an interpreter, knowing what the family members do not want to say.

So . . . what kind of comment does this text make on childhood? For me, it foregrounds the surreal nature of life, both for the child and the adult. The choice of locations are comprised of those which are physically possible to inhabit and those which are not, yet are inhabitable within the inner reality of life, the point where imagination, perhaps dream, and the emotional states of being come to fusion: the surreal. This text works very logically and rationally, yet has the capacity to move beyond such, not, I would suggest into fantasy, because the worlds are governed by a strict rationality, but into the surreal. What happens here is not "fantastic," although some of the locations themselves are beyond physical possibility. Childhood (and I believe, to a certain extent, adulthood) is about trying out new situations, new places to inhabit either physically or imaginatively. Those locations are determined by outside forces and by interior emotional states of being. "Nowhere" is perhaps somewhere we have all been at some time on our lives. Whether we decide to come back and where we come back to is crucial. Where this family comes back to is a house with three phones where they are constantly talking and engaging with each other, albeit at a distance.

What fascinates me about this text is the combination of the rational and the seemingly irrational. The defiance of the constraints of linear narrative and yet the strong sense of progression and joining in a journey. The question of the subject identity is in the strength of the narrative voice. There is a need for rhythm in the prose, for some ordering and the quiet way in which this family is observed. The emotional demands are quietly made. Each place has its own identifiable aesthetic and sensory atmosphere in both the illustration and the text, emphasizing the importance of awareness of the aesthetic which is highlighted in the prose and visually produced in the pictures. The positioning of the child narrator as an observer is also central to the text and the construction of identity. One learns through observation; one learns of love, and friction, quirky behavior, responsibility, and loss. Perhaps we learn also of that which is most fragile and that gives the greatest strength. The everydayness of life is here communicated through the surreal and what is emphasized is that security is needed, symbolized by finally moving into "our" house and no longer living in "Uncle's Hat."

References

Bauer, Jutta. *Opa's Engel* [Grandpa's Angel]. Paris, France: Gallimard Jeunesse, 2002. Print.

———. *Selma*. Geneva: La Joi de Lire Jeunesse, 2003. Print.

Breton, André. *Manifesto of Surrealism*. Tuscaloosa: University of Alabama, 1924. Web. 13 Jun. 2011. <http://www.tcf.ua.edu/Classes/Jbutler/T340/SurManifesto/ManifestoOfSurrealism.htm>

"Existentialism." *All About Philosophy*. Web. 13 Jun. 2011. <http://www.allaboutphilosophy.org/existentialism.htm>

Norton, Mary. *The Borrowers*. London: Dent, 1952. Print.

Stamm, Peter. *When We Lived in Uncle's Hat*. Illus. Jutta Bauer. Tunbridge Wells: Winged Chariot Press, 2006. Print.

Tutti Frutti Company. Web. 13 Jun. 2011. <http://www.tutti-frutti.co.uk/shows/uncle>

"Using Stories From Winged Chariot Press" *Winged Chariot Press*, 2006. Web. 13 Jun. 2011. <http://www.wingedchariot.com/docs/Uncle'sHat%20support.pdf>

"JINGS! CRIVENS! HELP MA BOAB!" – IT'S A SCOTTISH PICTUREBOOK

MAUREEN A. FARRELL

School of Education and Visual Journeys Research Term, University
of Glasgow, Glasgow, Scotland

*A nation's literature has traditionally been seen as a reflection of the values,
tensions, myths, and psychology that identify national character. In the construction of culture and identity there are many shared values that can be discerned
and revealed through story and literature. But no literary genre teaches us more
about a culture and its values than the literature published for a society's children. In Britain the concept of a literary national identity is further complicated
because the United Kingdom is made up of four separate nations and each
constituent part claims its own distinctive identity. Within children's literature
the picturebook "genre" presents an extremely rich context for the exposition of
national identity, using as it does both written text and images. This article
suggests that Scottish picturebooks are distinctive and challenge young readers,
especially Scottish readers, to discover and recognize who they are in the face
of mass market globalization in children's book publishing and thus presents
particular opportunities to examine issues of identity in both the cultural and
educational environment.*

In 1965 Nancy Larrick published a groundbreaking article called
The All White World of Children's Books in the Saturday Review of Books
(Larrick 1965). Principally aimed at the American market, this
article signaled the beginnings of inclusion of children of color in
children's literature, but initial portrayals were stereotypical and
contained widespread cultural inaccuracies. Through the 1980s,
there grew recognition of the importance of authentic accurate
descriptions of race and the role it plays in child development.

All this may seem very far removed from the portrayal of a distinctive Scottish identity in children's books, but despite the fact that Scottish authors and publishers were responsible for creating some of the most iconic children's books of the nineteenth and twentieth centuries, Scottish identity, and thus Scottish children's literature, was generally subsumed under the heading of English, rather even than British, literature.

As time has moved on the emphasis in children's literature has changed further to a preoccupation with multicultural literature and, despite controversy over its definition, it is this aspect that features in the discussion of what makes a Scottish picturebook. The well-known American artist and illustrator of children's books, Tom Feelings has stated that, "truly authentic, multicultural picturebooks are created—written and illustrated––by people belonging to the race, culture, or nation of origin which is reflected" (Feelings 1985). This is not the view commonly held in Scottish literature. Currently, post devolution Scotland finds itself embedded within a multicultural, international context and has a relatively flexible view of what constitutes a Scots person as detailed by its civic citizenship legislation, which values an individual's choice of residency as highly as their familial descent (Schoene 2007). Thus a counterargument contends that a Scottish children's book or picturebook may be generated by someone who belongs to the Scots culture *or* by someone who chooses to locate themselves in Scotland but who exhibits recognizably Scottish attitudes toward Scotland or the world at large. Either way the importance of distinctive, identifiable Scottish picturebooks becomes pivotal because:

> when children are involved with literature it not only allows them to see a world through a window applicable to their experiences but also allows them to see images of themselves in texts they encounter. (Smith 1997)

The title of this article includes the phrase "Jings! Crivens! Help ma Boab!"—an expression unlikely to be recognized beyond Scotland. But, generations of Scots will recognize the catchphrase of a character called "'Oor Wullie." The comic strip *Oor Wullie*, first appeared in the D. C. Thomson publication *The Sunday Post* in 1936, and has been running continuously ever since. It follows the adventures and misadventures of a small boy, 8 or 9 years old, with spiky blonde hair and black dungarees. He gets into trouble with his teachers and the local bobby, plays truant with his gang, breaks windows (*usually* by accident), fights the local bullies, torments "softies" and "'swots," eats huge quantities of sweets and food, and studiously avoids the romantic attentions of the local girls. Every episode begins and ends with Wullie sitting on his trademark upturned metal bucket. He is a young Lord of Misrule who embodies values of irreverence, friendship, and fairness.

Though Wullie is a character from a comic and thus rather on the edge of the picturebook continuum, his catchphrase encapsulates a specific issue for Scottish picturebooks and that is the issue of language. At the time the comic strip was first published, it was considered uncouth to swear or take the Lord's name in vain. But people liked to have exclamations for their exasperations. The exclamations used by Wullie are basically corruptions of religious terms and, as can be seen from this extract from a 1942 strip, Wullie was always under some pressure to clean up his language (see Figure 1).

This aspect leads to further consideration of how to define a Scottish picturebook. Does it, for example have to be written in the Scots language? Scots have access to three languages for our literature: Standard Scottish English, Gaelic, and Scots (of different varieties). A picturebook using any one of these three languages would comply with the definition of a Scottish text.

There are notions of Scottishness that seem to hold true in general, but using these would be to fall into the trap of

FIGURE 1 Oor Wullie © the Sunday Post D. C. Thomson & Co., Ltd. Printed with permission from D. C. Thomson.

essentialism. Scottishness has to be shaped and re-defined in a way that is compatible with the modern world: this requires maturity and confidence as well as knowledge and should not be irreconcilable with notions of tolerance and recognition of diversity. The kaleidoscope, known to the Romans but re-invented in 1816 by Scot Sir David Brewster, is a useful metaphor for Scottish identity itself. The elements that make up "Scottishness" may remain the same but they re-form into different complex patterns over time. Increasingly, contemporary Scottishness involves complicated negotiations among the various Scottish "'identities" that have proliferated since the 1970s and 1980s, and may include multiple identities. For example, someone could see themselves as a citizen of Glasgow, a Lowlander, a Scot, and a Briton. Using the following definition, picturebooks are identified as Scottish picturebooks that meet the following criteria:

> A Scottish picturebook is one that deals centrally with issues of life and experience in Scotland, is set in Scotland, or exhibits recognizably Scottish attitudes towards Scotland or the world at large. Material engages the reader in the identification of and reflection on the wide range of cultural communities and individual experiences which constitute a distinctive national culture. While mainly produced by Scottish writers, texts need not be limited to Scottish authorship; the experience of non-Scots living and working in Scotland or commenting on Scottish life and culture from outside, when coherent and substantial, can justifiably be regarded as a valuable contribution to Scottish Literature. Additionally, Scottish born writers can write material that is not overtly Scottish in nature but if told in their own true and unique Scots voice then it should be considered a Scottish text. (Farrell 2008)

One writer's work clearly fits into the first of these definitions. Mairi Hedderwick is a native Scot who lives and works on the island of Coll. She both writes and illustrates her own books and also illustrates the work of other authors. She is uncompromising in her commitment to overt Scottishness in her books. She uses the obvious symbols of tartan, bagpipes, highland cows, Shetland jumpers (sweaters), saltires, and so on. But, she also uses Scottish vocabulary, names, flora and fauna, locations, weather, food, music, and dance. This commitment has sometimes brought her into conflict with publishers who feel that this could limit her global appeal. Despite this, from the beginning, *Katie Morag* has captured the affection of children in and beyond Scotland. The first in the series, *Katie Morag Delivers the Mail* (Hedderwick 1984), was immediately seized upon as an excellent example of nonsexist children's fiction, mainly because of the dungaree-wearing, tractor-fixing Grannie Island. (Katie Morag's other grannie is known as Grannie Mainland and is a much more conventional, feminine character.) The stories are set on the fictional island of Struay, loosely based on the real island of Coll, and the author-illustrator's attention to detail in both text and illustration has reputedly resulted in requests for travel directions. Without direct comment, the books allow children to consider an island way of life and the differences in experience and values between mainland and island, urban and rural. Hedderwick is also extremely skilled at capturing and conveying incidents which are common experiences for children in any community or family group while still remaining true to recognizable experiences, rooted in Scottish culture.

One particularly effective collaboration of hers is with author and poet Tom Pow in *Callum's Big Day* (Pow 2003). This picturebook tackles the issue of Scottishness head on. With keen observation, humor, and not a little irony, author and illustrator foreground and explore stereotypical Scottish images ancient and contemporary, and poke gentle fun at the "shortbread tin" notion of Scottishness.

Callum invites all his friends to a party at his house, but the invitations contain one key instruction, "Dress Scottish." Callum has a very particular view of what it means to be Scottish. He wants to be "a REAL Scotsman like he'd seen in the films." The irony of this is not lost on contemporary readers who recognize that, especially the Hollywood vision of a Scotsman bears little resemblance to the reality. The story makes reference to the Selkirk Grace, the Highland Fling, William Wallace, Bannockburn, Bonnie Prince Charlie, Culloden, and porridge, all of which could be regarded as stereotypical Scottish images. But the final image of the party shows beautifully the humorous subversion of these stereotypes while at the same time acknowledging the cosmopolitan nature of Scotland in presenting new cultural combinations for modern Scotland (see Figure 2).

The illustrations include an Asian girl in a sari with a tartan sash, a Chinese girl with a tartan umbrella, a child inside a

FIGURE 2 Reproduced by kind permission of the illustrator (color figure available online).

Loch Ness monster costume and another dressed as a haggis, a black boy in a saltire tee-shirt and tartan cap and an Asian boy in full highland dress complete with turban and Indian drum. All of these show children responding to the instruction to "dress Scottish" but also show how children's imaginations can allow them to respond creatively to what the instruction means. This openly multicultural approach shows minority cultures and how characters interact with or live within the mainstream society.

Some writers and illustrators also use overtly Scottish images and references: Aileen Paterson, Linda Strachan, Natalie Russell, Richard Brassey, Andrew Wolffe, Munro Leafe, and Moira Munro, for example. These books are immediately recognizable as being Scottish either in their subject matter or location but questions can arise about whether they also place limits on Scottish identity.

Another group of writers and illustrators depend on Scottish folklore, language or reference to cultural icons like Robert Burns to establish their Scottish credentials. Itchy Coo, is a publishing company which produces books written in Scots language especially aimed at children and young people. The imprint was set up in 2002 and is jointly run by writers James Robertson, Matthew Fitt, and Edinburgh-based Black and White Publishing. Since

2002 thirty-six different titles have been published, in a variety of genres and including board books for "very wee bairns" to a major anthology of 600 years of literature in Scots for upper secondary students. They include the first ever Scots language publication in Braille and their most recent venture, the translation into Scots of works by authors such as Roald Dahl and A.A Milne. Picturebooks include a series of boardbooks about Katie including *Katie's Coo, Katie's Beasties, Katie's Ferm, Katie's Moose, Katie's Year* and *Katie's Zoo* (Fitt and Robertson 2008a).The format covers traditional rhymes with *Rabbie's Rhymes* (Fitt and Robertson 2008b) described as "Robert Burns for wee folk" a "keek-a-boo" book and a hide and seek book showing that all contemporary formats can be covered. The more conventional picturebook mode includes *A Wee Book o Fairytales in Scots* (Fitt and Robertson 2003), *Sweetieraptors* (Rennie 2002), a Scots counting book and alphabet book, illustrated collections of poetry including *Manky Mingin Rhymes in Scots* (Fitt and Robertson 2004), and a Scots retelling of the story of Hercules in *Hercules: Bampots and Heroes* (Fitt 2005). This translation remains completely true to the original story while the use of Scots language gives a unique Scots perspective. The synopsis offered describes it thus:

> When the great hero Hercules commits a terrible crime his father Zeus punishes him by making him the slave of his step-brother Eurystheus. To win his freedom back, Hercules must perform twelve seemingly impossible tasks or trauchles.

Bob Dewar's inspired illustrations are reminiscent of contemporary cartoon films in their sophistication, yet manage to add to the text and contain implicit humor: all aspects that conform to the recognized conventions of picturebooks.

Traditional literature, including folk literature, folklore, and fairytales also form an important group of picturebooks in Scotland. These tales feature the accumulated stories passed down, primarily through oral storytelling, and in Scotland's case especially through the ballads. Each tale type has characteristics that set it apart from other types and, when authentic, may add a description for cultural context, describe what changes may have been made to the tale and explain why the changes have been made. Folktales feature common people with characters who often seem "flat" because they are intended to represent every-man. These kinds of tales have tight plot structures filled with conflict; cycles of three often occur and elements of magic may be incorporated but logic rules, so the supernatural must be plausible within the context. Two examples of Scottish picturebooks in this genre are *Pirican Pic and Pirican Mor* (Lupton 2003) retold by Hugh Lupton and illustrated by Yumi Hco and *Tam Lin* (Yolen 1998) retold by Jane Yolen and illustrated by Charles Mikolaycak. The first is a Hebridean folk tale and the second a particularly well-known Scottish ballad. Interestingly, Hugh Lupton is an English storyteller and Yumi Heo hails originally from Korea, while Jane Yolen and Charles Mikolaycak are both American. Yet, these works clearly fall into the category of Scottish picturebooks because of the subject matter.

Pirican Pic and Pirican Mor tells the story of two friends who fall out over a pile of walnuts: one has eaten the other's share. "I'm going to find a stick and whack and thwack you for that" says Pirican Mor. But, revenge is not so quick or easy as it seems. The tree directs him to an axe, the axe to a stone, the stone to water, the water to a stag, and soon the whole landscape is caught up in the tale and Pirican Mor is drawn further and further from his moment of fury. This is a fine example of a cumulative tale and the illustrations are quirky, clever, and not obviously Scottish. The result is a tale that, while its origins are in the Hebrides of Scotland, could be located almost anywhere in the world providing an international flavor. Inspiration may come from Scottish culture but the thematic handling encourages acceptance of other traditions.

Tam Lin is a ballad that seems unique to Scotland not least because of its debt to native fairy lore. It is among a small set of ballads that are unusual because they have been adapted or re-told in novelistic form many times, particularly for young readers. Novelistic retellings of such traditional material became more common in the twentieth century and could be considered the twentieth century's unique contribution to the telling of traditional tales. Many ballads feature elements of loyalty, the supernatural, comedy, and fantasy. The characters in the original Tam Lin ballad engage in premarital sex, argue over abortion, human sacrifice, and magic. The stories often end with the curse of the Queen of the Fairies rather than a simply happily ever after. These characteristics, as well as a remarkable number of motifs associated particularly with Scottish fairy lore and a notably feminist perspective, make the ballad *Tam Lin* "perhaps the most important supernatural ballad of them all" (Briggs 1977) *and* among the more obvious choices for prose transformations. Yolen admits to always being fascinated by it, principally because it is one of the few—possibly the only one— where the woman does the rescuing. She has also said that in her retelling she tried to remain faithful to the oral tradition even to the point of reading it our loud as she worked. This retelling of an ancient Scottish ballad leaps from the page. Here, in all its moon swept mystery, is the story of how Jennet, red-headed daughter of the MacKenzie clan, rescues Tam Lin, the man she loves, from certain death at the hands of the Fairy Folk. . . . Mikolaycak's sensitive illustrations bring stirring, wistful overtones to the action and add rich depth of characterization to the protagonists. Yolen's story is lyrical and true to the spirit of the tale and time. Mikolaycak's large-format double-page spreads of vibrant watercolor and colored pencil on Diazo prints soar across pages and break out of slender, peaceful borders. The red and green of rose bushes dominate; the tartans are original designs–"After all, a faery tale demands its own colours and plaids," Yolen states in background notes. She omits Jennet's pregnancy and other adult aspects of the tale, but in all other respects this version remains true to the original tale. Mikolaycak follows Yolen's cues in the selection of his palette: green for the camouflage of Jennet's cape and red for the rose that is emblematic of the heart. On the cover is a vignette of a briar branch (the rose) and on one twig two gold rings entwined. On the front cover, the lovers are swathed in tartans against a full-blown rose. Facing the dedication page is a red rose on a thorny stem, just opening. A single-page illustration shows a frog and a snake emerging from an undergrowth of briars, and there are grass-green borders around the illustrations as a framing device. The ruined castle is in the distance. A single red rose appears when Jennet meets Tam Lin in his tartan of black and white. Mikolaycak orchestrates a careful interplay of color, form, and text. When Jennet returns she wears a mantle of green over a blood-red skirt and bodice so that the faeries won't see her. Tam Lin turns into a serpentine creature with gray-green scales that seem to emerge from his tartan, but then becomes a lion. Jennet bests the queen. Tam Lin's clothing has been burned away. She covers his nakedness with her costume. At the end, Tam Lin's black and white tartan is now embedded with a plaid pattern derived from the "MacKenzie" plaid, the lovers surrounded by roses in bloom. As with all the best picturebooks, the complex text/picture relationship should complement each other and the role of the reader/viewer should become incxtricably entwined with the verbal and visual patterns. In these examples of Scottish picturebooks, we have clear examples of how the picture/text relationship can result in different meanings for different readers but retain a recognizable Scottish flavor.

Another group of Scottish picturebooks are those which, rather than comprising a *representation* of a nation, are perhaps better described as more *representative* of the nation. These include Scottish authors and illustrators by birth or residence, whose work is not overtly or obviously Scottish. In this category, Debi Gliori, Ross Collins, Lynn Mercer can be included as examples. Here the Scottish element is much more subtle, if even obvious at all. Debi Gliori's *Mr. Bear* series, for example, presents a central character that she herself has described as "the unreconstructed Scottish male."

One of the pleasures of reading a picturebook from a particular country is that it retains a sense of place. But more importantly, multicultural literature in its most authentic form is an area of literature that focuses on the reality of various cultures, showing both the positive and the negative aspects. Once immersed in the work of authors and illustrators writing about or drawing images of their own cultural group, a reader has a solid basis for comparison with books by authors whose ethnicity is unknown. Thus, a recognizable and distinctive corpus of Scottish picturebooks helps readers recognize themes, topics, values, social conventions, and language—those elements that characterize a culturally specific body of literature.

Scotland was a separate nation until the Act of Union in 1707. After that, even as a "stateless nation," Scotland retained its own education system, its own legal system and its own national church. The critic Roderick Watson has observed, "the main 'state' left to a 'stateless nation' may well be its state of mind, and in that territory it is literature that maps the land" (Watson 1995). Scotland's new cultural policy was unveiled in 2006 and it gave Scottish

Literature a prominent place in the initiative. At the same time this document also acknowledged the importance of education in giving access to and highlighting Scotland's literary heritage. Both educational discourse and common sense tells us that it is reasonable to expect Scottish literature to form a significant part of the Scottish school curriculum and for Scotland's pupils to have access to it. The more recently published Goring Report (Goring 2010) calls literature "one of Scotland's finest indigenous arts," going on to say that, "a thriving literary culture is an important element in the well-being of the nation." The report also suggests that:

> Education is arguably the single most important element in nurturing and sustaining an intelligent and avid readership for Scottish Literature (and indeed *all* literature) . . . Reading for pleasure is every pupil's right, giving them an insight to their cultural heritage, allowing them to hear voices from their own background – or different – who convey Scotland's distinctive history, outlook and values. (27–28)

It becomes vital then to acknowledge the existence of a corpus of work that is recognizable as Scottish Children's Literature, including picturebooks, existing separately from but complementary to English Children's literature and which can be used in schools by teachers and read by children in order to explore and interrogate their own cultural history and identity. But, how do Scottish picturebooks become a repository for the formation of culture, identity, and nationhood and how does this impact on young readers?

It is in the stories written for and told to children that a culture confirms and reproduces itself. Literary reading begins where the reader is and goes on from there. Unless the reader finds him or herself in a book they will have a hard time finding anyone else. Children are in the process of learning to become members of the adult community they have been born into. To join that community they must learn its values—become the kind of people who can live within it by accepting and negotiating its particular visions of what kind of people they should be. To be shaped by one's culture is merely to be human, and Children's Literature is inevitably part of that which does the shaping. In turn, children's literature, including picturebooks, far from comprising a mere afterthought in Scotland's creative psyche, plays a fundamental role in the shaping of that collectively imagined space known as Scotland and the culture it seeks to represent. If it is true that in some sense children become what they read about, then the narratives that children are exposed to can play an important part in creating the "them" they believe themselves to be.

Post-devolution Scotland finds itself embedded within a multicultural, international context. The talk is now of "One Scotland: Many Cultures," that is, of national identity as a series of encounters and negotiations within the political fact of the state. Post-devolution, the hope is for a Scotland less defensive and less anxious, as well as one more open to multiple ways of knowing, being, and living. If that is the case then the question must be asked, are we advocating a plural Scotland, which implies respect for inherited boundaries and where individuals are located within one or another of a series of ethnoracial groups to be protected and preserved, or a cosmopolitan Scotland which promotes multiple identities, emphasizes the dynamic and changing nature of many groups and is responsive to the potential for the creation of new cultural combinations? Having made a strong case for the recognition of a cadre of Scottish picturebooks, the challenge now is to articulate how our picturebooks can continue to contribute to this important debate.

References

Briggs, K. *A Dictionary of Fairies*. Harmondsworth: Penguin, 1977. Print.

Farrell, M. A. *Cultural Identity in Scottish Children's Fiction*. Glasgow: University of Glasgow, 2008. Print.

Feelings, T. "The Artist at Work: Technique and the Artist's Vision." *The Horn Book Magazine* (Nov/Dec 1985): 685–94. Print.

Fitt, M. *Hercules: Bampots and Heroes*. Edinburgh: Itchy Coo, 2005. Print.

Fitt, M., and J. Robertson. *A Wee Book o Fairy Tales* (2nd ed.). Edinburgh: Itchy Coo, 2003. Print.

—. *King O The Midden: Manky*. Edinburgh: Itchy Coo, 2004. Print.

—. *Katie's Coo*. Edinburgh: Itchy Coo, 2008a. Print.

—. *Rabbie's Rhymes*. Edinburgh: Itchy Coo, 2008b. Print.

Goring, R. Literature Working Group Policy, 2010. Web. 16 April 2010. http://www.scotland.gov.uk/Publications/2010/02/17145942/1

Hedderwick, M. *Katie Morag Delivers the Mail*. London: Random House, 1984. Print.

Larrick, N. "The All White World of Children's Books." *The Saturday Review* 48 (1965): 63–65. Print.

Lupton, H. *Pirican Pic and Pirican Mor*. Oxford: Barefoot Books, 2003. Print.

Pow, T. *Callum's Big day*. Aberdour: Iynx Publishing, 2003. Print.

Rennie, S. *Sweetieraptors*. Edinburgh: Itchy Coo, 2002. Print.

Schoene, B., ed. *The Edinburgh Companion to Contemporary Scottish Literature*. Edinburgh: Edinburgh University Press, 2007. Print.

Smith, E. B. "Reflection and Visions: An Interview with Rudine Sims Bishop." *Journal of Children's Literature* 23.1 (1997): 66–68. Print.

The Sunday Post. Dundee, D. C. Thomson & Co., 1936. Print.

Watson, R. *The Poetry of Scotland*. Edinburgh: Edinburgh University Press, 1995. Print.

Yolen, J. *Tam Lin*. San Anselmo: Sandpiper, 1998. Print.

DO YOU LIVE A LIFE OF RILEY? : THINKING AND TALKING ABOUT THE PURPOSE OF LIFE IN PICTUREBOOK RESPONSES

JANET EVANS

Liverpool Hope University, Liverpool, UK

It is increasingly accepted that one can respond to picturebooks in a variety of different ways, however it is only in the last decade or so that some picturebooks are being recognized as extremely complex multimodal texts which often make great intellectual and cognitive demands on the reader. Picturebooks can be very powerful texts; they can stimulate rich discussion and release previously untapped thoughts and emotions allowing the reader to reflect on life and its vagaries. This article asks who is the audience for picturebooks that are challenging, controversial, and unconventional and outlines why it is crucial to read, share, and talk about them collaboratively. It describes how one such book, The Short and Incredibly Happy Life of Riley by Colin Thompson and Amy Lissiat, at first glance a seemingly simple, humorous text, was used with 10 and 11 year old children as the stimulus for some reader response work which quickly led to some profound, indeed, quite philosophical discussions about the purpose of life and the choices that human beings make as they exist in a material world.

> The whole book is like a puzzle, from the front cover to the back page. It is about Happiness versus Money. The man has more money than Riley but he's not happier. A lot of the time this is true because money can't buy you love or happiness. Therefore these characters are like people from the world now although the book was set a long time ago.
> Bonnie, 10 years old

This was Bonnie's response to Colin Thompson and Amy Lissiat's book, *The Short and Incredibly Happy Life of Riley* (2005). It shows some of her thoughts about the book when she was asked if it made her think of anything that was happening in the world about her at the time.

Some books are easy to read and do not seem to need much interpretation or deep thought to understand them. However, many books are more complex and some readers find them difficult to understand. This may be because of: the plot itself; the complexity of the characters; conflict within the storyline; the resolution (or lack of resolution); or it could even be a reader's differing background knowledge and cultural dissonance with what the text is saying. Such difficulties may apply to narratives, in general, but they also apply when we focus on picturebooks in particular. Just because picturebooks are shorter, have fewer words, and, of course, have illustrations, does not necessarily make them easier to read; in fact, many are extremely complex multimodal texts that often make great intellectual and cognitive demands on the reader.

If books can sometimes be difficult to understand how can we help readers to unpick,

comprehend, and, of course, enjoy what they read? Responding to texts through collaborative talk is the response that emerges again and again. A body of research has developed focusing on how children learn through talk (Corden 2002; Goodwin 2001; Jarrett
2006; Myhill 2006). In addition there is an increasing body of research focusing specifically
on how talk helps children to respond to and understand texts (Baddeley and Eddershaw
1994; Chambers 1993; Evans 1998; Graham 1990; Reedy 2006; Sipe 2008; Styles and
Bearne 2003; Watson and Styles 1996).

Sharing and Responding to Books

When reading picturebooks, I frequently feel the need to have someone to share them with,
someone with whom I can enjoy the books—enjoyment being one of the principle reasons
that most people read narrative picturebooks—but also, someone with whom I can feel
comfortable about asking tentative questions or sharing some of my thoughts, observations,
and queries in relation to the meaning of the book. The analogy of a journey has been used
many times to represent this notion of reading and understanding but it is a pertinent
analogy . . . reading a book from beginning to end *is* like a journey and it is good to have
someone to share the journey with you, someone to guide you and go with you as you
travel through the book and as you read the story. Metzger seems to be in accordance with
this journey idea and he gives us some indication of how easy and, at the same time, how
difficult the understanding of narrative books can be when he states:

> Stories go in circles. They don't go in straight lines. So it helps if you listen in circles
> because there are stories inside stories and stories between stories and finding your way
> through them is as easy and as hard as finding your way home. And part of the finding
> is the getting lost. If you're lost, you really start to look around and listen. Moral: be
> prepared to take risks.
> (Metzger 1979)

So, just reading the book itself is hardly ever enough! Evans (2009a) noted that it is the
shared oral responses and the ensuing discussions that allow fuller and maybe differing
understandings to take place. Think about the reasons that Book Clubs and Reading Circles, where people read books alone prior to discussing them, are so successful. It is the
enjoyment of talking about and responding to what has been read in a comfortable,
unthreatening environment with like-minded people that is one of their main successes.

Talking About Books... Collaboratively

How could this way of talking about and responding to books with others be emulated with
young children without the discussion becoming a mere question and answer session?
Kathy Short (1990) looked at the importance of book talk with children between the ages of
5 to 11 years old. She later stated that, "Children should enter the story world of fiction and
non-fiction to learn about life and make sense of their world, not to answer a series of
questions" (Short 1997, p. 64). Short gave the name *Literature Circles* to the way of
responding to and talking about books in small group, literature based discussions. Daniels
(1994) further developed this concept and showed how such groups could be used by teachers to encourage children to respond to books. *Literature circles* provide a very effective way
of enabling teachers and children to respond to picturebooks, but they are still not used
enough in classrooms! Many children read books alone without sharing them or talking
about them; this is hardly ever enough to enable in depth meaningful understandings to
take place!

Shirley Brice Heath (1985) shared this sentiment when, in her seminal text, *Ways With Words*, she stressed the importance of talk by stating, "For those groups of individuals who do not have occasions to talk about what and how meanings are achieved in written materials, important cognitive and interpretive skills which are basic to being literate do not develop." Similarly, Smith (2005) in her minibook, *Making Reading Mean*, stated that an approach to reading that focuses on the process and not just the product is needed, she emphasized that we have to, "get inside children's minds as they read, so we can see and guide the thought process" (22). Smith went on to say that the best way to do this is through talk. In commenting that children will emulate what they see and experience in their classrooms she noted that, "Children who experience talk used in an exploratory and reflective way to think about texts and reading will begin to use that sort of talk themselves. Participating in talk can induct children into new ways of literacy thinking" (23).

Talking about and responding to books in differing ways can include written responses (Hornsby and Wing Jan 2001), drawings and illustrated responses (Anning and Ring 2004; Arizpe and Styles 2003), role play, dramatic enactments, and Readers' Theatre (Dixon et al. 1996), and non-verbal responses to include gestures, eye movements, and touch (Styles and Noble 2009; Mackey 2002). These differing ways of responding to reading all enable fuller understanding to take place; however, it is sometimes the time between readings that allows fuller understanding to develop; this is where our brains are given opportunities to process information. Arizpe and Styles (2003) noted this and found that much of the understanding that children make of books goes on in the thinking and the talking about books, often between re-readings of the same book. Of course we have to recognize the rights of the reader to not respond at all and to read a book quietly and without interruption Pennac (2006). Many people prefer to read silently but there are also many readers who relish the opportunity to talk about what they have read during and after their read.

Who are Picturebooks For?

Talking and responding to picturebooks with other interested readers is one way to develop fuller understanding. However some picturebooks are complex, controversial, and difficult to understand, sometimes with subject matter that is deemed by some to be unsuitable for children, and I have often found myself asking who such picturebooks are written for and exactly who is the audience for this kind of picturebook? Would young children make sense of them? Would older, fluent readers perhaps dismiss them immediately without taking a second look simply because they have pictures as Smith found when sharing picturebooks with 10 and 11year olds who were not used to responding to such texts (Smith 2009). Are they bought and read by adults as works of art as opposed to being simply books with pictures and narrative storylines (Evans 2009b)? Exactly who is the audience for some picturebooks?

In writing about a very early Edward Ardizzone book, one which was published in 1937 and which courted much controversy as a result of its subject matter, perceived at the time as being unsuitable for children, Rebecca Martin (2000) posed this exact same question. She asked, "Who is the audience of children's books – children, adults or both? How are these audiences different? Is the picture book today just for small children? (243). The Ardizzone book about which Martin was writing was *Lucy Brown and Mr. Grimes* (Ardizonne 1937). In brief, the story is about a friendship which develops between an orphan girl (who lives with her aunt) and a lonely old man. They meet in the park and he gives her presents when she asks for them. Eventually after the orphan girl helps him to recuperate from an illness, he formally adopts her and she lives with him and his housekeeper in a beautiful country house. This was Ardizonne's second title and in contrast to his first provoked outrage among American librarians who censored it at the time. The book went out of print and was not reissued for 33 years. The censorship was based on perceived issues of stranger danger (the little orphan girl goes away with an old man, Mr. Grimes), potential paedophilia (even in the thirties), and being rewarded for exhibiting bad manners (Lucy is adopted and is showered with gifts of every imaginable kind by her new parent, Mr. Grimes). However one reacts to *Lucy Brown,* the fact is that it was originally written for children.

These kinds of reactions raise questions about picturebooks that challenge the child reader (by dealing with subject matter such as sex, death, adoption, suicide, disability, etc.). Should such books be read alone by children or should adults be available to discuss and respond to the kind of questions which will inevitably be asked? Martin asks, "Do small children need more help distinguishing between fact and fantasy? Are they likely to do whatever they see or read about in books, such as talking to strangers?" (249). There is evidently still much debate about whether children should be protected from these kinds of issues in books. However, the fact remains that these and other sensitive and emotional issues can be dealt with if adults are available to discuss any questions or queries which may arise. The importance of responding to books is crucial to enable children to make sense of books at all levels of complexity; whether *Lucy Brown* was a book which was "ill conceived" or not is immaterial to the fact that children need to be given the opportunity to talk about and respond to texts.

The Short and Incredibly Happy Life of Riley. . . A Polysemic Picturebook

Of course, the subject matter of the books needs to be suitable in terms of reader engagement. *The Short and Incredibly Happy Life of Riley* is one such book (see Figure 1).

FIGURE 1 Front cover of *The Short and Incredibly Happy Life of Riley* by Colin Thompson (color figure available online).

This book is a humorous but at the same time thought provoking multimodal picture-book which, in a wonderfully symbiotic blend of words and pictures, compares the parallel lives of a rat and a human. The concerns this book raises are not apparent at first but as one reads, re-reads and talks about the book the complexities emerge and the subtle and yet very clever way in which Thompson has woven twenty-first century issues into a seemingly simple picturebook are uncovered. It is a multilayered, polysemic text that almost demands to be read and responded to with other readers. The children noted this almost straightaway:

Louis: You wouldn't understand this book if you read it on your own.

Katie: Yeah - if you read the book with other people you'd get loads more ideas and the different ideas make you agree and disagree.

Louis: When we found out about the "It's my alias - Amy Lissiat bit" we knew that the whole book was a puzzle.

Charlie: Mmm - every page is a riddle!

Katie: . . . and sort of like a video as well - you have to keep rewinding to understand - like when we read and re-read to understand the book.

Holly: Even though the book is so short it's so long as well so you have to keep going back, before moving on. To get ideas in your head you have to keep moving forward and back.

Riley the rat is very happy with his life but sadly rats do not live long. Conversely, Norman the human is enormously unhappy with his life; he is dissatisfied with just about everything and constantly wants to be someone else, with somebody else, doing something else in a different place. And yet, of course, human beings live a lot longer than rats!

The book is an allegory; one part dealing with a simple life of contentment, the other looking very cynically at a life led by consumer capitalism, a life gone mad with pure greed and unnecessary indulgence. The book is quite obviously delivering messages about accepting who you are and trying to be happy with what you have in life. Therein lies the quandary! How does one live life to the full? Life on earth is for real, not a dress rehearsal and one has to make the most of it or risk unhappiness and an unfulfilled time on earth. Norman the long living human seems to have been drawn into the consumer lifestyle almost without knowing and without knowing what to do about it.

Throughout the book Thompson plays with our senses and our emotions; intertextual references are made in relation to works of art, music, cult personalities, popular culture concerns, and up to the minute current issues. He also draws on the reader's awareness of idioms, proverbs, metaphors and word play, and in order to understand and fully appreciate the text, the reader is obliged to draw on many of these different perspectives through their previous experiences. Even the title refers to the saying, *Living the life of Riley* by which is meant an easy and pleasant life.

The peritextual information in the book informs us that Colin Thompson created it jointly with Amy Lissiat. For those who know Thompson's previous picturebooks, it comes as a surprise to see a very different illustrative style has been used; a style which is sketch like and cartoony, making use of collage, photo images, and computer graphics, a style that renders the book fully multimodal in its use of different media and modes.

Thompson normally writes and illustrates his books alone so an emerging first question is in relation to Amy Lissiat. Who is she and why is she co-creating this book with Thompson? The back dust jacket flap intriguingly states:

> Amy Lissiat was born in France in 1920 and has worked as an artist's model, poet's muse and an international imagination consultant. In 1955, on her way to Tristan de Cunha by hot air balloon, she made a forced landing in Australia. She has lived here ever since, although for the first fifteen years she thought she was in Patagonia. She now lives in northern New South Wales.

Lissiat's stated date of birth made her 85 years old when she worked on the first edition of this book and her colorful, attention-grabbing life style demands that questions be asked of her authenticity. Does she really exist or is she a figment of Thompson's imagination? Further research shows that Amy Lissiat, an anagram for, "it's my alias," was Thompson's alter-ego!

Thompson is playing games with his readers, teasing them and urging them to dig deeper to discover the complexities of this seemingly simple, yet somewhat incongruous and convoluted picturebook. It is more than evident that the complexity of this picturebook should not be underestimated

Children's Thoughts, Discussions, and Responses

It was while reading and talking about *The Short and Incredibly Happy Life of Riley* with a class of 10 and 11year old children that its complexity as a multimodal, multilayered picturebook became increasingly apparent. The children were used to reading and sharing all kinds of picturebooks along with offering viewpoints before, during, and after reads. They were also very much aware of how this kind of reader response activity frequently helped them to fully appreciate a book, indeed Hannah (11 years old) commented:

> When we start to talk about a book in a group I love it because we start with one thing and then end on something totally different. We turn the pages and really start to think about different things. I really like that and I always ask myself, "How did we get on to this from that?"

Pre-Reading Prediction

Prior to reading the book and before any discussion, the children were asked to predict what they thought it might be about, initially having just the title, then having the front cover illustration in addition to the title. As expected the predictions were simple one-liners, however even at this pre-reading stage the predictions showed that the children were beginning to anticipate what the book might be about.

With the title only, Holly commented, "I think the book is about a boy named Riley who has a fun and adventurous life. But at the end he dies."

When the front cover illustration was shown in addition to the title she went on to say, "Now I think it is about a man named Riley who gets drunk and he meets a mouse and they become friends."

Responses to the Book after First Reading

After the first joint reading of the book and a whole class discussion, the children were asked to talk and write what they felt it was about. There were differing views but a similar theme ran through their oral and written responses . . . that of making a choice between a good life and a bad life; many of the children felt there was a moral in the book. Holly's views were typical:

> I think this book is about how bad life can be and how good it can be depending on what you choose. This picturebook is about good life and bad life and how the man is trying to follow Riley's good life. The stains (in the illustrations) represent how ungrateful and careless he has been. The sticks represent how he has been hurt, not just in violence, but in many different ways. It is even more painful trying to get rid of them. People are starting to turn their backs on him and that is making him even more depressed. Later on in the book he decides he is going to change but was too late, his life was coming to an end and he couldn't enjoy his life for as long as he wished for.

> The moral to this book is that you can choose which path you take, the good life or the bad life. But if you choose the wrong one you will never be able to change.

> Holly, 10 years old

Empathizing with the Characters

After discussing what the book was about, the children looked more closely at characteristics of the two main characters. By entering the persona of each character, they used speech bubbles to express what Riley and Norman might think of their own personal lives.

"I'm Riley and . . ." (see Figure 2).

I'm Riley and this is
what I think of my
life at the moment...

- I have a great family, a wife and lots of children

- I don't complain about things because there are
  always small and little things that I can live with.

- My favourite food is cheese and my favourite place
  is my home.

- I live my life to the max and don't look back to
  find things I could improve

- I like colours and fun.

- I have basic things and a comfortable bed.

- I am generous, happy, cheerful and kind.

FIGURE 2 Riley speech bubble (color figure available online).

"I'm Norman and . . ." (see Figure 3).

I'm Norman and this is what I think of my life at the moment...

- I am stressed and fat, no one wants to be my friend
- All my friends have stuck sticks in me and broke my heart, I'm lonely.
- All the women laugh and make fun when I give them a rose.
- I don't care about the way I eat, what's the point?
- I feel drowned with bad memories, I feel as if I could die.
- I am always wanting new things but still not happy when I get them.
- I am not wanted and that means I am lonely which makes me more miserable.
- I am ashamed of my life.
- I am depressed, I try calling for help but it seems like nobody hears me.
- I hate my life, it has been depressing and I am not happy.
- My thoughts are driving me round the bend I can think of things but I can't seem to find courage to do them.

FIGURE 3 Norman speech bubble (color figure available online).

After considering what Riley and Norman might think of themselves and their own life-styles the children started to wonder what they might think of each other. A thought bubble response sheet was designed and the children used it to record Norman and Riley's thoughts about each other. It was evident that they were more than capable of empathizing with the characters' feelings and emotions and most of the children portrayed Riley as the happier, more content character who was at ease with himself and his life. Norman, by contrast, was portrayed as a rather sad, lonely, and depressed character who did not have any friends and had many personal and social problems despite his material possessions (see Louis's view Figure 4 and Bonnie's view Figure 5).

FIGURE 4 Louis' thought/response sheet (color figure available online).

Norman: I think that Riley has brought fun to my life. Riley is my only friend as well as Bert. I love how Riley is so kind. He introduced me to his massive family. It is very cosy. All my family live some way away. I like Riley! (Louis)

Riley: I think Norman could use a bath. He is depressed and lost in his soul. He is shaky so he spills his coffee all over the place but he just doesn't have any friends. He is a kind man but has had a hard life; he just needs lots of friends to help him through his life and misery. Other people think he's dreary from his looks but I'm going to help him. (Louis)

What does Norman think of Riley's life?

I think Riley is really cool. He has a wife and children and friends. I am so jealous because he has a great personality and he has gone far with his life. Riley's home is pretty large and can hold lots of people other than his family. He has a very smiley face. I wish I was him. I wish I could have a lot of friends like him.

What does Riley think of Norman's life?

I think Norman is an ill man – depressed, he could do with a bit of my life for a while. He has no friends except his innocent dog called Bert. He gets bullied because he isn't like the other people but he is hanging around with the wrong kind of people. He is disheveled on the outside but kind on the inside.

FIGURE 5 Bonnie's thought/response sheet (color figure available online).

Norman: I think Riley is really cool. He has a wife and children and friends. I am so jealous because he has a great personality and he has gone far with his life. Riley's home is pretty large and can hold lots of people other than his family. He has a very smiley face. I wish I was him. I wish I could have a lot of friends like him. (Bonnie)

Riley: I think Norman is an ill man—depressed, he could do with a bit of my life for a while. He has no friends except his innocent dog called Bert. He gets bullied because he isn't like the other people but he is hanging around with the wrong kind of people. He is disheveled on the outside but kind on the inside. (Bonnie)

Text to Life . . . Links with World Happenings and Current Events

Moving on from the issues that emerged from the initial discussions, the children were asked if the book made them think of anything that was happening in the world at that moment. This question was rather like opening a dam. It instigated a long discussion that was very philosophical at times and which certainly highlighted once again the children's ability to empathize with others less fortunate than themselves and to link with the current affairs of the moment. Holly's response showed a clarity of thoughts which was both inspirational and moving in its depth:

Colin Thompson's book reminds me of . . . the recession! The world is in a mess for most people. The book made me think about recent happenings in the world—the World Cup. Spain has been paid millions of pounds for winning a few games of football. Players in the UK are being paid over £100,000 per week whilst people are struggling to pay for food.

How is the UK managing to pay for the footballers' wages whilst we are in a recession?

Why are footballers' wages still so high when there are people forced to live on the streets?

These are the questions I want answering.

Also happiness and Riley. How can Riley be so happy with nothing and the footballers are unhappy yet they get paid £100,000?

The world is turning to greed and maybe if there were a few more Rileys the world would be a better place.

Emily's succinct points clearly showed her understanding of the concerns being considered:

Thompson's book reminds me of:
• the poverty that is all around us,
• the recession and all the debt that we owe,
• the credit crunch,
• the thought that this is how the world is run and how unfortunate but how very true this is,
• that there are families that have too much and could give up something to help out the world,
• all the money that Spain won (40 million pounds) could have gone to charity and all the other many causes mentioned above.

So basically, the book reminds me of the amount of mess we are in!

Toward the end of the book, Thompson reiterates that humans always want what they cannot have but they usually live a long time whilst rats such as Riley are happy with their lot but only live a very short time. He concludes, "This is why it is never a good idea for people to compare their lives to animals. You will only end up feeling depressed . . . because realizing that rats have a better life than you do, is really, really sad. And the answer is very simple really – you just have to be happy with a lot less" (n.p.).

Release Your Inner Riley

The last page of the book concludes with a simple statement, "Release your inner Riley" to accompany the text. Norman's coffin is seen with Bert, his dog, in attendance, and two rats in and around the coffin (see Figure 6).

FIGURE 6 "Release your inner Riley" the last page in *The Short and Incredibly Happy Life of Riley.* Permission granted by Colin Thompson (color figure available online).

The children were asked what they felt Colin Thompson meant when he said, "Release your inner Riley." Their views showed their understanding of the fact that to be happy in life we often need to make do with a lot less in terms of material possessions and to appreciate others for what they are. They responded to Thompson's text both at a superficial, surface level and at a deeper, more philosophical level and they frequently related back to points of view that had been presented by their peers during their class and group discussions. Various interpretations of the phrase were offered.

Louis summed it up succinctly:

> It means that you need to live life to the full because you won't get another life. Don't ever complain about what you've not got because when you get it you will only want more and more.

Katie went into more detail:

> It means that "Riley" is a feeling of happiness inside you that sometimes we forget about. And sometimes when you get sad and lonely you should be happy and look on the bright side and remember the "Riley" inside of you (release him) in a way that will let people know you're happy with your life and what you've got.

Holly too gave a more detailed and somewhat reflective interpretation:

> Happiness! Everyone has it inside them but there is an easier option, sadness. That seems silly; I mean who would choose sadness over happiness? But to be unhappy with something, which everyone is, is choosing sadness. To release your inner Riley is to dig deep, think about what you say, and to be content with anything and everything. This is hard but it makes everything so much easier.

> Riley represents happiness. Norman represents sadness.

Does the Book Have Anything to Tell Us?

After its release in Australia this multimodal, polysemic picturebook was awarded the 2006 *Picturebook of the Year* by the Children's Book Council of Australia. In addition, as an excellent example of a cross over book (Beckett 2012; Falconer 2008), it soon became a cult book; a book that adults wanted to have for "special," thought provoking, older birthdays where one starts to think about the reasons for being alive! The fact that it is a picturebook simply adds to its allure. It represents a particular "take" on life; a take, or view which urges the reader to take stock and think about the purpose of life; almost an existential view when one considers that how Norman lived his life was defined by his actions and interactions with his immediate world and by his own set of standards rather than any kind of external moral code. The existential views of Jean Paul Sartre and his contemporaries led me to remember the famous, much earlier quote by Rene Descartes who in 1637 wrote, "*I think therefore I am.*" Was Norman's life real or not; was Colin Thompson linking Norman's life to reality or to a mere set of perceptions and preconceptions about reality and the consumer capitalist life many of us lead in the twenty-first century?

Of course this is for the reader to respond to and decide.

Using this book with 10 and 11-year-old children made me realize once again how very powerful picturebooks can be; they can stimulate rich discussion and release previously untapped thoughts and emotions allowing the reader to reflect on life and its vagaries. Katie summed up the sentiment behind the book in quite a poetic manner:

> Life is like a rollercoaster—full of ups and downs. Riley has the ups and the man has the downs.

Release your inner Riley could well become a catch phrase for experiencing life to the full; maybe we should all do it more often!

Note

More information about responding to books can be found in *Talking Beyond the Page: Reading and Responding to Picturebooks*, Janet Evans (2009) Routledge.

References

Anning, A., and K. Ring. *Making Sense of Children's Drawings*. London: Open University Press, 2004. Print.

Arizpe, E., and M. Styles. *Children Reading Pictures: Interpreting Visual Texts*. London: Routledge Falmer, 2003. Print.

Ardizonne, E. *Lucy Brown and Mr. Grimes*. London: Oxford University Press, 1937. Print.

Baddeley, P., and C. Eddershaw. *Not So Simple Picture Books*. Staffordshire: Trentham Books, 1994. Print.

Beckett, S. *Crossover Fiction: A Genre for All Ages*. London: Routledge 2012. Print.

Chambers, A. *Tell Me: Children, Reading and Talk*. Stroud: Thimble Press, 1993. Print.

Corden, R. *Literacy and Learning Through Talk*. Buckingham: Open University Press, 2002. Print.

Daniels,H. *Literature Circles: Voice and Choice in the Student Centred Classroom*. Maine: Stenhouse Publishers, 1994. Print.

Dixon, N., A. Davies, and C. Politano. *Learning With Readers Theatre: Building Connections*. Portage & Main Press, 1996. Print.

Evans, J., ed. *What's in the Picture: Responding to Illustrations in Picture Books*. London: Paul Chapman Publishers, 1998. Print.

—. "Reading the Visual: Creative and Aesthetic Responses to Picturebooks and Fine Art." *Talking Beyond the Page: Reading and Responding to Picturebooks*. London: Routledge, 2009a. pp 99-117. Print.

—. *Talking Beyond the Page: Reading and Responding to Picturebooks*. London: Routledge, 2009b. Print.

Falconer, R. *The Crossover Novel: Contemporary Children's Fiction and its Adult Readership*. London: Taylor and Francis Ltd, 2008. Print.

Goodwin, P. *The Articulate Classroom: Talking and Learning in the Primary School*. London: David Fulton, 2001. Print.

Graham, J. *Pictures on the Page*. Sheffield : N. A.T. E., 1990. Print.

Heath, S. B. *Ways With Words: Language, Life and Work in Communities and Classrooms*. New York: Cambridge University Press, 1985. Print.

Hornsby, D., and L. Wing Jan. "Writing as a Response to Literature." *"The Writing Classroom: Aspects of Writing and the Primary Child*. Ed. J. Evans. London: David Fulton, 2001. pp 46-65. Print.

Jarrett, P. "Time to Talk Sense." *The Primary English Magazine* 12.2 (2006). Print.

Mackey, M. *Literacies Across Media: Playing the Text*. London: Routledge Falmer, 2002. Print.

Martin, R. "Edward Ardizzone Revisited: Lucy Brown and the Moral Editing of Art." *Children's Literature in Education* 31.4 (2000): 241–57. Print.

Metzger, D. "Circles of Stories." *Parabola*, IV.4 (1979): 104–105. Print.

Myhill, D. "Talk, Talk, Talk: Teaching and Learning in Whole Class Discourse." *Research Papers in Education* March (2006): 19-41. Print.

Pennac, D. *The Rights of the Reader*. London: Walker Books, 2006. Print.

Reedy, D. "Effective Talk in Reading Lessons: Having Proper Conversations with Children." *English 4 – 11* 28 (Autumn 2006): p 21. Print.

Short, K. *Talking About Books: Creating Literate Communities*. Portsmouth: Heinemann, 1990. Print.

—. *Literature as a Way of Knowing*. Maine: Stenhouse Publishers, 1997. Print.

Sipe, L. "Young Children's VisualMeaning-Making in Response to Picturebooks." *Handbook of Research in Teaching Literacy through the Visual and Communicative Arts*, Vol. 2. Eds. J. Flood, S. B. Heath, and D. Lapp. London: Lawrence Erlbaum, 2008. Print.

Smith, V. *Making Reading Mean*. Royston: UKLA Publications Minibook 20, 2005. Print.

—. "Making and Breaking Frames: Crossing the Borders of Expectation in Picturebooks." *Talking Beyond the Page: Reading and Responding to Picturebooks*. Ed. J. Evans. London: Routledge, 2009. pp 81-96. Print.

Styles, M., and E. Bearne. *Art, Narrative and Childhood* . Stoke-on-Trent: Trentham Books, 2003. Print.

Styles, M., and K. Noble. "Thinking in Action: Analysing Children's Multimodal Responses to Multimodal Picturebooks." *Talking Beyond the Page: Reading and Responding to Picturebooks*. Ed. J. Evans. London: Routledge, 2009. pp 118-133. Print.

Thompson, C., and A. Lissiat. *The Short and Incredibly Happy Life of Riley*. Australia: Lothian Books, 2005. Print.

Watson, V., and M. Styles. *Talking Pictures: Pictorial Texts and Young Readers*. London: Hodder & Stoughton, 1996. Print.

READING MENTAL PROCESSES IN *THE ARRIVAL*

BRENDA BELLORÍN

Language and Didactic Literature Studies Department, Unversitat Autònoma de Barcelona, Barcelona, Spain

MARÍA CECILIA SILVA-DÍAZ

GRETEL Research Group, Universitat Autònoma de Barcelona, Barcelona, Spain

Wordless picturebooks show the possibilities and limitations of visual narratives. Mental processes—such as perceiving, thinking, longing, remembering, and feeling—usually call for verbal representation since they cannot be depicted visually, as they are part of the character's interiority and not of his or her external appearance. However, visual narratives find ways to depict these processes by leaving gaps for readers to fill in with their previous knowledge and hypotheses. Framing, the use of close-up, colors, and sequencing, are some of the devices used by the author to convey what is more often expressed through words. This article explores the representational strategies that Shaun Tan uses in The Arrival by looking into responses to the book from a group of native and immigrant children in Catalonia, as recorded in 2008 in the context of the international research project "Visual Journeys."

Hidden Intentions

Recognizing characters' intentions is a key to understanding narratives. Intentions drive characters' actions and reveal conflicts and obstacles that may prevent them from achieving their goals.

This study has been made possible thanks to the financial assistance of the Spanish Ministry of Education and Science for research projects I+D: EDU2008-02131/EDUC. Thanks to Martina Fittipaldi for sharing her transcripts and her thoughts with us about the children's responses.

However, because intentions belong to the realm of mental processes, making them visible in a picturebook is not an easy task.
The difficulty extends to all mental processes. By mental processes we understand everything that takes place in the characters'
mind: perception, introspective thinking, emotions, and dreams.
Characters can verbalize intentions, the narrator can reveal them
to the reader, but they can only take shape in the realm of
action once characters initiate actions towards achieving their
goal. Verbal language is an ideal means to expressing perception through verbs like "listen," "see," "smell," emotional processes
(desire, fear, hate), and cognitive processes (believing, knowing, thinking), and, in that sense, visual language is less adept
than written text at expressing the character's mental processes.
Intentions, for instance, must be conveyed by showing the actions
that motivated them or by illustrating the fulfillment of the goal.
Readers can only infer intention by relying on previous knowledge or on what the images suggest. That is why multimodal texts
such as comic strips resort to convention like the speech bubble
to introduce thoughts; in film, thoughts tend to be expressed as
an inner voice that the viewer can listen to, but that the rest of
the characters are not aware of (voice off). In wordless narratives,
mental processes are implied through gestures, actions, and, in
some cases, through more sophisticated visual strategies that, be
as it might, require the active participation of the reader to fill in
the indeterminacies.

In this article we will explore the visual strategies that can
be used to suggest intentions and the ways in which readers recognize and reconstruct intentions that have not been expressed
through text.

Narrating with Words, Narrating with Images

Kress and Van Leuwen argue in *Reading Images, the Grammar of
Visual Design* (1996) that visual and textual structures are not
interchangeable means of representation: each medium has its
own expressive possibilities and limitations. In other words, some
elements are better conveyed through text and others through
images. According to Kress (2003), images leave fewer gaps
to be filled by the imagination: what needs to be represented
is represented. Writing, in contrast, conveys elements that are

relatively empty of visual detail, such as emotions, thoughts or the passing of time. In other words, images tend to have a greater degree of specificity: the detailed look of a character can be depicted in a condensed manner that leaves almost no space for ambiguity. Such extent of detail, though, would require many words and would still be subject of ambiguity. However, verbal language is usually more effective (in a succinct way) at expressing movement or the passing of time than images are, since the latter require sequencing or other graphic strategies to convey such detail.

To overcome these "limitations," there are certain conventions in the ways multimodal texts distribute meaning between text and images. Mitchell (2000) asserts that "in the case of comics, the normal relationships between text and images can be conventional, with a clear division of labour" (234) —we expect thoughts to be represented through speech bubbles, movement through the sequencing of panels on the page, and so on. On the other hand, Mitchell believes that picturebooks exhibit rather flexible and experimental relationships, with a "high degree of tension between text and images" (234). Their interaction is such that it is sometimes difficult to clearly differentiate their responsibilities in the representational division of labor. Evidently, Mitchell's assertion is not valid for all comic books or all picturebooks, but it does, however, address certain trends in both multimodal genres. In ground-breaking picturebooks, the experimental text-image relationship tends to be stressed even more, and conventions of other multimodal texts, such as comics, cinema, website or other forms of screen layouts are incorporated.

What If Pictures Do All the Storytelling?

Picturebooks that exclusively rely on images to tell a story— wordless picturebooks—follow their own conventions. Nodelman (1990) wrote that his five-year-old son, a very proficient reader, could describe actions while reading a wordless picturebook, but could not say what motivated them. In this regard, a wordless picturebook is distinguished by the fact that it can easily show action but not emotion and meaning (190). Nodelman argues that stories without words create a distance between the reader and the characters—not being able to know what is going on in their minds, the narrative perspective is concealed: "They tend to tell the stories that depend on distance rather than involvement . . . the pictures tend to be in a cartoon style that exaggerates not only the actions for the sake of clarity but also the appearances for the sake of humor" (Nodelman 188). Thus, contrary to what is widely believed—that visual narratives offer many interpretations and that everyone can come away with their own story—Nodelman believes that for this kind of narrative to work, it must be "tightly controlled in every respect" (192).

Intentions Revealed: The Expression of Mental Processes in *The Arrival*

The Arrival is a good example of a densely sequenced visual narrative. It challenges Nodelman's idea that a wordless picturebook should be a simply-plotted story represented in a cartoon-like style. Tan adopts a style closer to realism, yet distant from it because of the surreal and fantastic elements displayed. The narrative is truly complex, involving intertwined stories, a non-lineal temporality that includes the use of flashbacks, and so on. The story deals with convoluted situations with great emotional weight that need to be conveyed in a blunt and convincing way. In spite of the story's complexity, Tan opts not to distribute functions verbal and visual language—in fact, written language in his story has been depicted in an imaginary alphabet that is impossible to read and, therefore, becomes part of the visual language.

In the international research project "Visual Journeys: Understanding Immigrant Children's Responses to the Visual Image in Contemporary Picturebooks," *The Arrival* was discussed with different groups of children, many of them immigrants. The responses of children in Barcelona show how the participants deduced the motivations of the main character even though these were not made explicit by the text. After looking at the beginning of the book, the children concurred that the protagonist leaves behind a hostile reality and migrates to a new place in search of better horizons: work opportunities and a better life for his family. The readers recognized the character's intention and allowed themselves to add their own hypotheses about how long he would stay and whether or not he would bring his family.

Calvin: Because if he didn't like it, he would not have come. And if he
has, it's to bring his family, too, to have a better life.

Alan: Maybe not. Maybe he just wants to have a job.

Martina: What do you think, Naima?

Naima: That he came to have a job.

Alan: He can work two years to . . .

Naima: To bring his family as well, like Calvin said. [1]

The book encourages readers to elaborate hypotheses of this kind. To tell the story Tan employs a layout in vignettes, as comic books do. The high degree of sequencing displayed in the book allows him to tie the story together. Tan sets out to narrate through images without renouncing the complexity that can be achieved through text. An example of this is the panel (Figure 1) in which the character expresses his intentions by drawing a bed in his notebook to communicate that he is seeking a place to stay. By using an image within an image, Tan recreates a sort of visual "quote." The quote reveals the character's intentions and also allows the reader to infer the character is a newcomer, unable to speak the language of the place.

Other mental processes are expressed in *The Arrival*. Let's explore how and see what the children had to say.

Perceiving

The senses of smell, taste, touch, and hearing can only be suggested in images and, as Kress and Van Leuwen (1996) note, the

---

[1] This transcript, as well as the others, corresponds to the pilot of the Project "Visual Journeys" in Barcelona, Spain. Eight sessions were held in the School Ferrer i Guardia of Sant Joan d'Espí from January to March of 2008, with twelve children: six from Catalonia and six from abroad, all them between 11 and 12 years old. The foreign children were from different backgrounds: four were Latin Americans (Bolivia and Ecuador) and one from Morocco and one from Rumania. The interviews and discussions were held in Spanish. The transcripts have been translated into English by the authors of this article. The names of the children have been changed to protect their privacy and pseudonymous have been used instead. The Catalan children have been named: Carles, Emma, Xavier, Andreu, and Carolina. The immigrant children have been named: Alan (boy from Ecuador), Beatriz, Gisela, and Adrián (children from Bolivia), Calin (boy from Rumania), and Naima (gril from Morocco). The original transcripts are available in Martina Fittipaldi's M.A. dissertation (2008).

FIGURE 1 A visual quote that shows the character's intentions (color figure available online).

only processes of perception that can find an unequivocal equivalent in visual discourse are those belonging to the field of vision. Gazes, for instances, can be well conveyed through images, allow-

can be shown in the act of looking (in fact, the depiction of glances is a crucial element in visual narration) but smelling a certain scent, feeling something through touch, or listening to music cannot be fully conveyed. However, Tan manages to make visual metaphors of these processes of perception by appealing to the readers' ability to understand body language. In the double-spreads in which the protagonist is subjected to an unpleasant physical exam upon his arrival, touch and hearing are depicted by using close-ups of certain body parts: on the first page (Figure 2) the panel with the opened mouth almost makes it possible to hear the character saying "Aaaa," while others showing the examiner's hands touching different parts of the body convey the awkward-ness that the character must be feeling throughout this invasive procedure. On the second page (Figure 3), the character's inabil-ity to understand the questions of the examiner and the distress he feels at not being able to communicate properly is also shown through body language.

Remembering

Three characters tell the protagonist about the harsh experiences they lived through in their homelands that prompted them to migrate. These stories are introduced through flashbacks, sug-gested through body language and spatiotemporal changes. They are also expressed through variations in color and texture, as well as a different framing in the illustrations. All of these variations enable readers to understand when the characters are inhabiting a story that belongs to the past —when they are reliving memories— and when they are in the present recalling what happened to them in their countries of origin. As one reader said:

> I also know it's another story because of the color —as if . . . [pointing out to a different illustration with different colors] here it's like reality, there it's the past.

A different child uses her knowledge of how memories and thoughts are depicted in comic books by establishing an analogy with Tan's use of frames in his book:

> Here the frames show when it's a dream, they make it look like a cloud, it's like another type . . .

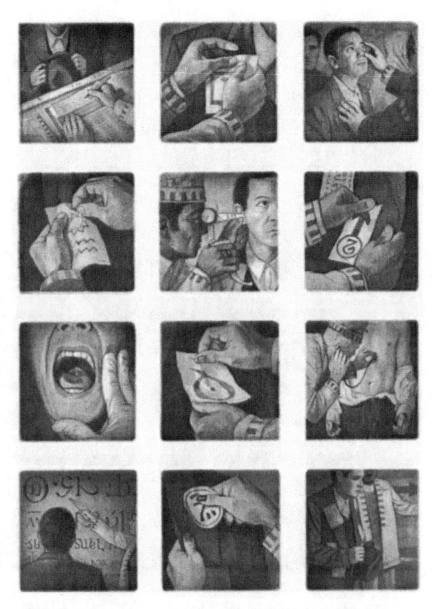

FIGURE 2 Awkwardness conveyed in images (color figure available online).

Not all of the readers where able to recognize in the spreads what (frames and colors) implied memories, flashbacks, and so on, but they were capable to tell that the images belong to the past in spite of their inability to point out which was the graphic index.

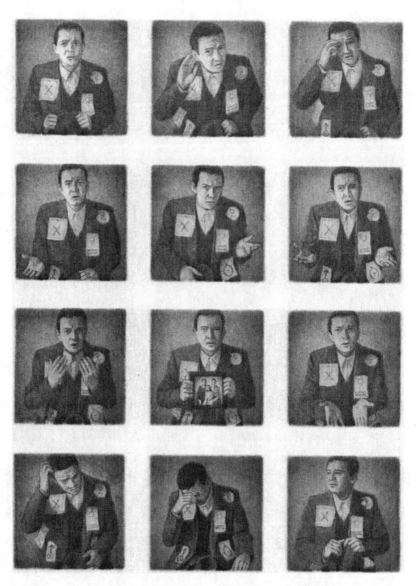

FIGURE 3 Distress and lack of communication expressed through images (color figure available online).

Martina: I ask you how you realized that these pages contain the life of
   these people?
   Beatriz: Well, maybe because the protagonist does not appear.
Martina: And only because of that, only because the protagonist does not
   appear?
   Calin: Yes.

In this regard, it is relevant to ask whether color, layout, and
frames are triggers that help the readers to distinguish between
the current story and the remembered story. That is, if it is
perceived even if not consciously so.

Thinking

On several occasions, the readers verbalized what the characters
were thinking, often in a direct manner as if they were giving the
soundtrack of the narration, filling in the silence. Looking at the
panel (Figure 4) in which the man is sitting on his bed looking
at a picture that is clearly a family portrait, Carles said: "I wonder
how they are doing?"

The same boy said while looking at the spread (Figure 5) with
the sequence that portrays the girl having breakfast: "The girl in
the fourth window is looking, looking to one side, not to the bowl
of cereal, she is looking at the suitcases, thinking 'this is the last
time I am going to see my father's suitcases until he finds a job.'"

Longing

On more than one occasion the main character is shown writing.
The first time is during the trip on the boat, when the man folds
what he has written into a paper bird. The image is evocative:
the unintelligible writing—a writing that imitates ours but cannot be deciphered by us—opens a gap that the readers can fill in
with their own hypotheses (Figure 6). Martina, the teacher, takes
advantage of this to start a discussion on whether the protagonist
is writing down his desires or recording his experiences.

Martina: Hmm . . . and what is he writing on that paper that he folds into
   a bird?
   Emma: His wishes, what he desires. Martina: Good. She says his wishes.
   Do you think he is only writing down his wishes?
   Hilda: And his experience, right? The experience of being there, or of
   thinking, "what is all this? There was none of this back in my
   country." You know?

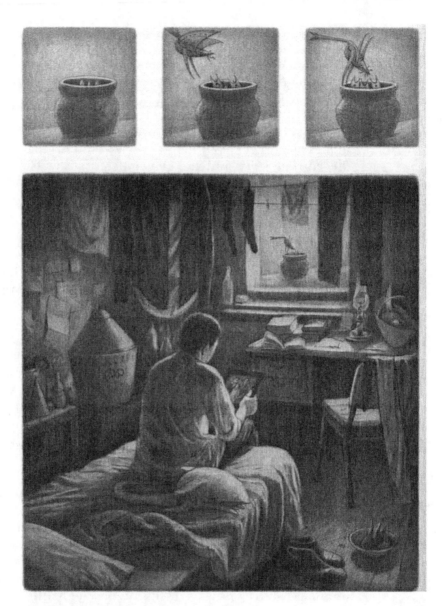

FIGURE 4 Spread that suggests the character's inner thoughts (color figure available online).

Feeling

Although emotions are usually conveyed with words, images can certainly suggest them. Resorting to the characters' body language

FIGURE 5 Sequence showing the girl's anticipation of the father's journey (color figure available online).

is only one of the strategies that graphic artists can use to express emotions. Other means of representation can be used for depiction, such as the character's surroundings expressing his inner emotions, or the development of sub-plots that function as

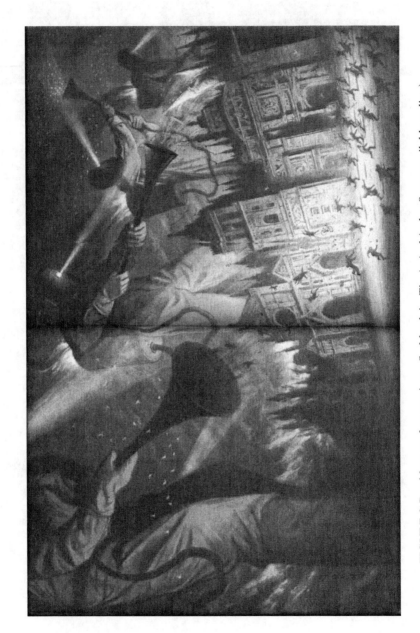

FIGURE 6 Doublespread conveying a flashback in *The Arrival* (color figure available online).

symbolic co-narratives that express the character's feelings. The readers of *The Arrival* interpret the use of color and the surrounding elements as an index of the emotional state of the main character. In the following excerpt we can see how the emotional state is associated with the use of color.

> Martina: And here, what does it remind you of? The form? The colors?
> Beatriz: Let's see, I'd say that by the colors, it seems very old, very old, from a long time ago . . .
> Calin: It shows the sadness, I say sadness because they are immigrants.

Another reader interprets one of the vignettes sequencing according to the scenery, to the clouds that appear:

> Emma: That, it's alternating and it shows the changes in the man's mood . . . normal, doesn't put a face in each image, he makes that the man . . . when there are lots of clouds he is depressed and when there are none he's excited and so on.

Likewise, some objects or images can represent metaphorically the character's feeling (Fittipaldi 2008), such as it is conveyed in the images of the dragons stalking the protagonist's city. For Calin, these images represent "like fear, like sadness—like hethe father is leaving, well it can be represented like fear or: the sadness of the daughter and the wife."

Meta-Linguistic Awareness

After reading and discussing *The Arrival*, children were made to reflect on the limitations of visual language. Alan pointed out that "through the illustrations you can see how characters are on the outside, but words tell us how each one is on the inside." Nonetheless, they also recognized that the limitations of visual language had been overcome by the author, since the children were able to discover core information in the story and elaborate on it, in spite of the book being entirely wordless, aside of course the back cover, the title and copyright pages.

The Case of "As If . . ."

The story is told through images. The paradox, however, is that the reader retells it through verbal language. There seems to be a tacit understanding that this is a translation, an interpretation. The constant use of "as if" seems to highlight the fact of reading images. On the one hand, there is awareness that what is depicted is not necessarily understood in the same way by each reader; that a text can be cross-examined and doubt can arise, that reading is a process. On the other hand, there is the understanding that this form of expression allows us to fill in spaces, give voice to the characters through citation. That is to say, the "as if" alludes to a distance and allows for the subordinate clause to form a direct quote, giving voice to the character. The "as if" is the license that allows the reader to become the spokesperson of the story. The reader assumes this narrative function when they take possession of the characters' voices:

> Gisela: It's as if they were telling him, "have a good trip."
> Calin: As if saying they have not passed one of the tests because he brings something, and he shows them the photo of the family: as if telling them, "I have a family to support —I need this job."

In this sense, readers assume the role of the verbal narrator, as Alan expresses when he reflects on the specificity of reading images: "All of us, all of us, all of us were not even reading or looking at the book—in the end, we were writing the story." Readers understand that they are in front of a different kind of narrative, which relates differently to reality, and must be read accordingly. They learn that images establish a different relationship to external referents; that the viewer, the beholder, must make some adjustments between his or her internal view of the world (Lowe 83), as in fact they do when they hypothesize about the setting:

> As if he goes from a very ancient era to a very modern one, or as he came to a very develop country, you know.

The readers also pick on that a wordless picturebook resembles other types of visual narratives and use their knowledge of the conventions of these other multimodal texts to grasp what is being "told" in the story:

> Gabriela: So that we can see the character's movement in few seconds
> Naima: for example, here we are seeing tu-tu-tu (makes sounds representing the movement of the protagonist)
> Beatriz: The fastest . . . and see what he is doing, right?
> Martina: Good, yes.
> Calin: The way he does it is as if it were a movie.
> Martina: It's as if it were a movie, Calin says.
> Calin: but without talking.
> Alan: mmm - I'm going to look some more.
> Martina: but without dialogue. Good.
> Alan: this reminds me of some . . . this reminds me that . . . no, nothing, nothing.
> Martina: Yes, say it. What does it remind you of?
> Alan: It's just that this is like the old movies, where they didn't talk but they were seen.
> Beatriz: silent film
> Martina: silent film.

They also become aware that they can read in other ways, that reading is much more than depicting letters. Visual narratives require readers to co-author (perhaps more than other narratives) the text because understanding what happens and what the characters are thinking and feeling has to be put into words. Some of the children were very apologetic about reading wordless picturebooks. One of them said:

> It would be . . . it would be a good way to read a book and imagine things, what the images are like, and imagine what would happen, and what they would be saying.

And another boy, Andreu, trying to describe the differences between visual and verbal language and to explain the necessity of co-authoring, said "with illustration you can see how characters look on the outside but with letters you can say how they are in the inside.

Overall, the different sessions with this group of pupils showed that a complex picturebook as *The Arrival* can succeed at expressing mental processes, as the children stated in their last session when they were trying summarize what they thought about the book:

> Emma: A book of drawings.
> Martina: Okay, a book of drawings . . .
> Carles: Without words.
> Hilda: That expresses many emotions. It's very emotional because any gesture, anything, is already telling you what is being felt.

References

Primary Source

Tan, Shaun. *The Arrival*. New York: Scholastic, 2007. Print.

Secondary Sources

Fittipaldi, Martina, "*Travesías Textuales: Inmigración y Lectura de Imágenes.*" Diss. Universitat Autònoma de Barcelona, 2008. Print.

Kress, Gunther. "Interpretation or Design: from the World Told to the World Shown. *Art, Narrative and Childhood*. Eds. Morag Styles and Eve Bearne. London: Trentham, 2003. Print.

Kress Gunther, and Theo Van Leeuwen. *Reading Images: The Grammar of Visual Design*. London: Routledge, 1996. Print.

Lowe, Virginia. *Stories, Pictures and Reality: Two Children Tell*. London: Routledge, 2006. Print.

Mitchell, W. J. Thomas. *Picture Theory: Essays on Verbal and Visual Representations*. Chicago: The University of Chicago Press, 2000. Print.

Nodelman, Perry. *Words about Pictures: The Narrative Art of Children's Picturebooks*. Athens: The University of Georgia Press, 1990. Print.

CROSSING VISUAL BORDERS AND CONNECTING CULTURES: CHILDREN'S RESPONSES TO THE PHOTOGRAPHIC THEME IN DAVID WIESNER'S *FLOTSAM*

EVELYN ARIZPE and JULIE MCADAM

School of Education and Visual Journeys Research Term, University of Glasgow, Glasgow, Scotland

Flotsam (2006), the award-winning wordless picturebook by David Wiesner is about the power and mystery of photographs but, at the same time, it plays with many of the techniques of photography to tell its story. This article discusses these themes and techniques and also examines children's responses to the picturebook, both oral and photographic. It considers photography with children as a research tool for investigating identity, culture, and literacy. The discussion about Flotsam *and the photographs provided an insight into children's understanding, not only of wordless narrative but also of the techniques and uses of photography. We argue that the photographs increase the children's control of the way in which their space, as well as their identity, is represented to others; a representation that is particularly important for immigrant pupils. We conclude that Flotsam can act as an incentive to reflect on the idea of looking carefully; to think about artistically complex texts and about the potential of photography. Finally, we suggest that photography is a promising way of exploring the visual image, not only from an investigative but also from a pedagogic point of view, as it can draw attention to the construction and metalanguage of image and thus strengthening comprehension and critical literacy skills.*

There are many picturebooks that use photographs as their principal medium or that combine illustration and photography, using the latter to create a more "realistic" impression. It is also evident that many picturebook artists have been influenced by the medium of photography. Much could be written about these border crossings; however, this article is about one of the few picturebooks that deal with photography as a theme—and does so brilliantly, as testified by the many awards it has gained, including the prestigious Caldecott medal. Equally, this article is about children's responses to this theme, both oral and photographic, and about using photography with children as a research tool to find out about identity, culture, and visual literacy.

Flotsam (2006) by David Wiesner is about the power and mystery of photographs but it also plays with many of the techniques of photography to tell its story and uses them to go beyond the borders of reality and fiction. In this wordless picturebook, children from different countries find a working camera that has washed up on the beach and use it to take photographs of themselves. They then send the camera back on its journey to other children around the world, creating visual connections across time and space, but not before they have seen some of the fantastic photographs that reveal secrets about the camera's journey.

In 2003, Mike Sharples et al. cited unpublished market research by Kodak which suggested that "over three quarters of children aged 6 years and older living in economically developed countries own or have use of a camera" (2). Given the wider availability of mobile phones with cameras, this figure must by now be even higher. As early as the 1970s, Gisèle Freund ended her seminal study on photography and society by noting that photography "has become the most common language of our civilization" (187). Again, how much more so now that with one digital click adults and children can send photographs anywhere in the world or post them online for anyone to see (and thereby raise a host of other issues)? New technologies have modified cameras and viewing options and thus modified the use and value of photographs. Most adults and children take them for granted and, as in the case with picturebooks, assume that their language can be understood at a glance, unaware that photography "mediates what it records, and constructs what it wants us to see" (Moss 2001, 289). They also have few opportunities to explore the social, cultural, and artistic complexity that can underpin the construction, interpretation, and potential of an image.

The idea of photography as a common language, the accessibility of digital cameras, and the knowledge children already have about photographs make it an obvious medium of communication for children who struggle to express themselves through oral or written language, particularly those who have recently arrived in a new country and culture. However, the *Visual Journeys* project was concerned not only with finding helpful ways for children to respond to complex picturebooks but also with developing strategies that could strengthen their comprehension and critical skills by encouraging them to go beyond the "literalness" of image and reflecting on how meaning is made through pictures.[1]

We were well aware of the potential of using picturebooks to enhance understanding of both text and image but also to increase language skills and to stimulate creativity (Arizpe and Styles 2003; Evans 2009; Pantaleo 2008a; Sipe 2008). *Flotsam* seemed an ideal picturebook for a project with communities of diverse readers many of whom had been on life-changing journeys between countries as it deals with the power of the visual image, journeys, and children from different times and countries. The picturebook's wordless nature led to an exploration of meaning making from narrative images and eliminated the difficulties a written text might pose for struggling readers. However, it was the first time that the project team had worked more closely with using and analyzing response to picturebooks through photographs.

In what follows, we start by reflecting on the picturebook's photographic themes and the techniques related to photography. We then discuss, first, the children's oral responses to these theme and second, the photographs taken by the children themselves. We consider photography both as a research tool for finding out about identity, culture, and literacy and as a strategy for responding to picturebooks and promoting intercultural communication.

A "Photographic Journey"

Wiesner is an American children's book author and illustrator whose picturebooks, *Tuesday* (1992) and *The Three Pigs* (2002), had

[1] *Visual Journeys* was funded by grants from the Faculty of Education, University of Glasgow and from the United Kingdom Literacy Association (UKLA). The other wordless text that was used in the project was *The Arrival* by Shaun Tan and although it is not "about" photography, many of the images were inspired by early photographs and the whole book can be read as a kind of photograph album.

already gained him two Caldecott Medals before being awarded yet another one for *Flotsam*. In this picturebook a young boy discovers a barnacle-encrusted underwater camera which has washed up on the shore. On closer examination he discovers a reel of film inside that, when developed, show fantastical images that no human eye has seen: moving cities on the shells of live turtles, an octopus in a lounge chair reading to a group of different sea creatures, a clockwork fish among a school of real fish. And yet, there is one more surprise, even more astonishing than these surreal scenes: the camera has journeyed not only through the depths of the ocean but through time, hiding in its last photo a visual timeline of children from around the world who have shared the camera's secrets.

Like the images in a wordless picturebook, photographs usually have no accompanying text; however, unless they are meant to be seen in some kind of sequence, unlike a picturebook, there is no sustained overall narrative. Wiesner has always been intrigued by what comes before and after the captured image. His books somehow convey the sequence of thoughts leading up to and following each picture and that quality explains why they are frequently described as cinematic. The storyboard construction for animated cartoons is brought to mind in *Flotsam* and this gives it that cinematic quality. There is a moment, however, in the middle of the book when the film inside the underwater camera is developed, and a succession of embedded "photographs" represent images that are unconnected to each other except for the fact that they were all the result of the camera's watery journey. This part of the book is not "cinematic" but "photographic" and it halts the overall narrative, forcing the reader to look closely at each of the "photographs"—just as the protagonist does.

The references to cameras and photography and the wordless nature of the text and the images themselves all point to the real theme behind Wiesner's picturebook, the importance of looking: "Characters, or eyes, look out to the reader towards, or through, something else, and challenge us to notice not just what is depicted but the very notion seeing itself" (Smith 2009, 87). The first, strong, indication of this theme is the full-page illustration of some sort of sand crab and an enormous eye behind it which, as it turns out, is that of a boy observing the creature through a magnifying glass. However, even before this there are clues on the cover (or under the dust jacket and at the flap if it is a hardback edition), the endpapers, frontispiece and title page that refer to the importance of looking, the most evident being the tiny camera reflected in the eye of the fish on the front cover. Turning the pages, we see the protagonist looking through a magnifying glass, a microscope, and the camera lens and sometimes we look with him, joining him in the surprise and pleasure of what he sees. We also see the eyes of different creatures and how our human eyes look to them. We look at things from different and unusual angles and perspectives and we catch glimpses of other worlds and other stories.

Both Sylvia Pantaleo and Vivienne Smith have written in detail about the central use of frames in *Flotsam* and about how understanding their function is necessary for a more in-depth interpretation of the picturebook. Pantaleo (2008b) argues that eyes, the multiple optical lenses and even the photographs within the photographs function as framing devices, intensifying the reader's focus. Smith notes that Wiesner's use of such detailed realistic images acts as a "conceptual framework" for the underwater fantasy photographs, "because the surreal is framed and embedded so firmly in real life, it seems both more plausible and more shocking. What if, Wiesner seems to ask the reader, the world is not so solidly ordinary as we imagine?" (87). The borders between reality and fantasy thus become blurred and the reader slides easily into the photographic stories within the story. This is also emphasized in Marcela Carranza's detailed analysis of *Flotsam* where she argues that because the artist uses "the techniques and expressive possibilities" of the medium itself:

> . . . it shouldn't surprise us, then, that Wiesner's book proposes photography as a pathway to access the marvelous, the impossible, that which is outside reason. In *Flotsam*, the photography (its simulation through the illustration) testifies about that which is beyond the real, the rational, the possible and the known. (Carranza 2010, EA transl.)

"Looking Deeply into the Picture": Children's Responses to the Camera and Photographs

One of the aims of the *Visual Journeys* project was to examine the visual literacy knowledge and practices of children with different cultural backgrounds and how these were brought into their understanding of complex wordless picturebooks. Researchers worked with 18 pupils in two Glasgow primary schools; aged between 10 and 11, some were "native" Scots and others came from countries such as Russia, Poland, Iraq, Congo, Afghanistan, Uganda, Pakistan, and Somalia. Sessions on *Flotsam* took place about once a week for 6 weeks during which small groups did a "walk-through" of the picturebook page by page; annotated images from the book; drew a "graphic strip" about a journey they had taken; and took photographs. Initially developed as research tools, we found that these strategies provided the children with different pathways for building on and sharing each individual's literacy skills and experiences.

Photography became a topic in the discussions around *Flotsam* when readers reached the spread which shows the boy discovering the camera on the beach and the next spread, which shows him asking people about it and taking the film out. However, the most perceptive of the children quickly related the picture of the camera to the slightly distorted image in the fish eye on the cover of the dust jacket and this caused great excitement and a return to look more closely at this image. Although there were a few suggestions that it might be a treasure box or a radio, it was very quickly confirmed to be an "old" underwater camera, with the barnacles indicating it had been in the ocean for a long time. There was discussion about how it worked and to whom it belonged. Some speculated that the camera had been taking a picture of the fish at the moment depicted on the dust jacket, a speculation that was confirmed later, when the film was developed. There was also speculation as to what pictures might be in the camera. Finally, there was some discussion about whether the spool of film was a "battery" or not and also about what the boy was doing in the shop ("he was buying another battery") revealing that many of the children had only ever experienced digital photography.

The first "photograph" plunges the viewer into an ocean world full of living, moving creatures as well as unexpected surprises. Immediate reactions to the "robot fish" made reference to the world of video and film: "it looks like a video and he's recording from his eyes" and "I think they're making a film because it has like robotic bits and pieces." We know that children bring their visual knowledge to help them make sense of complex picturebooks like *Flotsam*; throughout the sessions there were many references to visual media: photo albums, film sets, videos, and actual films such as *Finding Nemo* or cartoons like *Sponge Bob Squarepants*. Because many of these references were shared, they enriched the collaborative meaning-making task.

The children moved on to the boy's reaction which they interpreted as they followed the zoom out into the boy's face and the close up of his eye: "He's quite surprised by them . . ." (Susan). Mazim made a clear connection between the act of "deep" looking suggested by the large eye and "finding out" through details and clues, just as Mazim is doing himself. The words he puts into the character's mouth reflect the moment when the frame of reality is broken by the fantastic:

Evelyn: It's interesting how he's put that big eye there.

Mazim: I think he's finding out. I think he's trying to look deeply into the picture to see what those pictures are, and why there is so many pictures and he's looking at the details and clues . . . yeah, looking deeply inside . . . he's looking at that one and he's saying "mm, that can't be real because there's a machine . . ."

From this point on Mazim develops a theory that these photographs are constructed "film sets" (for a film being made for children) until he gets to the picture of the girl holding a photograph. When he looks at the photograph of what seems to be the first child who had the camera, Mazim says "so this is where the mystery begins" and once again the photograph becomes a key into the inexplicable connection between reality and fantasy.

Once alerted to the photographic theme, the children noted the borders that identified the images as "photographs." They noticed the cameras that appear in the "photograph" of the aliens who are on some kind of underwater safari and they wrote speech bubbles for the alien photographers with phrases like "Say cheese!" They speculated on who or what had taken the photographs and where the camera would have to be in terms of the angle and perspective. They commented on the change from color to black and white in the last photographs, explaining it meant that the photographs went "back in time." They were surprised when the boy throws the camera back into the sea and lets the photographs float away, rather than keeping them. They followed the camera's journey toward a new child, imagining what the various animals like the penguins and the whale might have thought about the camera and what new pictures it was taking.

Toward the end of the book they commented on the camera as the connection between one child and another. Nadia said, "it's kind of like a nice boy sharing with other people what happened in his life." Two of the thought bubbles the children wrote for the girls who appear in the last set of photographs read: "Good luck to the next person who gets my picture. I hope you get my picture" and "I'm going to try to give this to someone else so they can see me." During the sessions some children voluntarily brought in other family photographs and talked at length about them to the other children who displayed a great interest in looking at and asking questions about family members, places, houses, and other objects.

Children's Photographs as Research Tools

For the final task, children were asked to take photographs of the things, places, and people that were important to them in their life in Glasgow. The children were excited by the idea that they were to imagine they were going to throw their camera into the ocean so other children around the world could see their pictures. We were interested not only in *what* they would photograph but also *how* they would do it and whether they would incorporate any of the features we had been discussing throughout the picturebook: perspective, angles, color, shade, and pattern, among others.

While photography has been a common feature of ethnographic research for some time, there have been relatively few studies in literacy or education that make use of photographs taken *by* children. These "informant-produced images" are usually meant to allow child participants to have some control over the communication of their own "voice." or "views" in this case, or to provide data in ways which otherwise could be intrusive. However, Sarah Pink (2007) stresses that these images do not hold "intrinsic meanings" they are only made meaningful when the photographers talk about their intentions in taking the photograph and what the image depicts (89). Gemma Moss (2001) found this to be the case in her study on the gendering of reading which used photographs of reading activities in the home taken by children. Although the methodology provided Moss with data about this topic, she warns that the images can be deceptive and that it is important to ask questions about what they mean, rather than "read them at face value" (289). In another study it was children's talk about their photographs, along with the images themselves, that revealed to Marjorie Orellana (1999) which urban landscapes were meaningful to them.

Two other studies exemplify how children's photographs and children's talk about them can be used in different ways. Sharples et al. (2003) were concerned with children's photographic behavior and their attitudes to photography. Interviews were conducted with a selection of the180 children aged 7, 11, and 15 who participated in the study across five European countries and were asked to take any photographs they wanted over a weekend. Researchers established it was important to consider children's photographs from three angles: "as an aesthetic experience, as socio-cultural activity, and as a cognitive developmental process of increasing control of oneself and others" (13). They also identified differences in the content of the photographs and in the intentions of the photographers across the three age ranges. One of the study's main conclusions was that "children's photographs are not just their 'view of the world' but are also a construction of their identity in relation to their parents and their peers" (16).

During a pioneering study in Mexico Sarah Corona (2002) gave disposable cameras to children and adolescents living in a remote indigenous Huichol village and spoke to them about their photographs. Her aim was to understand visual forms of communication among subjects from a predominantly oral culture who had had almost no experience of the photographic, televisual or filmic image. Her analysis of the 2700 resulting photographs revealed, among other features, a correspondence to the forms of communication characteristic of the indigenous Huichol culture in which they were produced. Thus, for example, human and animal bodies are always represented whole in their art and craft, and this was extended to their photographs of whole bodies set in a background that reflected their geographic context and cultural activities.

These studies all raise interesting issues about "child-produced images" such as children's views about photography;

their handling of the cameras; social expectations; cultural constructions of image and the ethics of using photography as a research tool. It was not our original intention to explore these issues in this project, but they certainly arose and will be discussed briefly in the following section.

The Photography Task

Simple digital cameras were loaned to the children for a weekend with instructions to take photographs of objects, places and people that were important to them and/or images that they would like to share with a child living in another country. The quantity of photographs each child took ranged between 2 and 68. At the end of the task there was a presentation session where each photographer showed and talked about their images to their peers, the teachers and researchers through a PowerPoint presentation. Finally, they chose two images that were to be printed for them to keep.

Ethical issues were particularly relevant to this study given that half of the pupils belonged to a vulnerable group of refugee children and their families. Throughout the project we were aware of the need for sensitivity when discussing experiences of travel and migration and even more so in dealing with photographs. On one hand, we were concerned about having images of people and did not want to cause anxiety by asking the families for permission to make the photographs public; on the other, we felt it would be limiting if they could not take any pictures of people. In the end, the children were encouraged to take photographs of anyone and anything they wanted and these were shared only in the classroom presentations. For purposes of research dissemination only persons in public spaces or who could not be recognized would be shown.

The Analysis

A detailed visual analysis was beyond the scope of the project but we carried out a simple analysis based on three main features: photographic content, visual elements and themes related to the *Visual Journeys* project–immigration and journeys, and literacy and cultural references. For the first and second we adapted some of the categories used by the studies with children's photographs mentioned above (particularly content classification) and from textbook photographic analysis (aspects such as angle, texture, light, composition, pattern). The three features are interrelated and many of the categories are overlapping but for the sake of clarity, we have described the findings in three sections.

Photographic Content

The first level of analysis, photographic content, has been adapted from the coding schemes used by Sharples et al. (2003) and considers context and subject matter. There was a balance between photographs taken indoors and out of doors with most of the indoor ones taken at home or at school and three boys using the camera from inside moving vehicles. All photographs except for the safari park and the cow field were taken within an urban environment, mostly within Glasgow. Sadia took pictures of flowers and trees in the park near her home while Sara focused on the urban landscape: buildings, streets, and the playground. Within these, her subjects included cars, lorries, a fire truck, street signs, and bins.

The subject matter included all the categories mentioned by Sharples et al. (2003): people, animals, buildings, man-made objects, nature, and sports. Not surprisingly, it is people that matter most to these children: their family, friends, and community members populate most of their photographs. Photographs of people were the largest category and included both adults and children—mainly siblings, younger cousins, and school friends. The adults were mostly family members, although there were several photographs of school helpers such as teachers, the janitor, and kitchen staff.

There were also various "self-portraits" or "self-portraits with friends," or of themselves taken by others, doing sports, for example. The children are almost all smiling, but many of the adults, particularly from the immigrant families, are not (Orellana, 1999 and Corona, 2002 have also noted the solemn faces of adults who have not adopted the modern Western custom of smiling at the camera). Most "people" photographs are not formally posed, some children are making "silly" faces, and most appear to be aware that they were being photographed. There were quite a few photographs of pets. Objects included cuddly toys, shoes, books, mobile phones, digital and audio equipment, photographs, posters/billboards, buildings, ornaments, books, and food.

Mazin spoke excitedly about his trip to Belfast and some of his excitement is reflected in the photographs that tell the story of his trip. The photographic journey begins at the bus station; we see the bus station, the empty parking spaces, and then the bus driving up. There are photographs from the bus window. Mazin told the group he was "amazed" at the fact that the bus drove onto the ferry and at the facilities aboard the ferry: the lounge, the game machines, and the sea, all to be seen in his pictures. He then took several photographs of Belfast streets and buildings and of the trip back to Glasgow. Mazin's use of the camera creates a detailed narrative of the spaces he encountered on his journey, in strict chronological sequence; however, it was the words and the manner in which he described his photographs to the group that conveyed his amazement and excitement, allowing his audience to "accompany" him as he relived his experience.

Visual Elements

For the most part, the photographs reveal a direct approach, where the subject is confronted in a straightforward manner. There are no unusual angles and only a few close-ups, mainly of people's faces or objects. The backgrounds give the impression that they were simply those that the subjects happened to be in at the time of the photograph, such as the classroom, the bedroom, the sitting room, and the garden. With a few exceptions, the photographs are representational, the intention was that of documenting an image in response to the task, with neither an attempt to portray a more artistic or experimental composition nor to consider features such as contrast, framing or angle. Perhaps their level of expertise meant that it had not occurred to any of them to take pictures from anything but a face on position.

Only a few children took photographs that went beyond this "documentary" intention. Several of Samma and Sara's photographs reflected a more conscious intention to capture patterns.

Samma's patterns are from textiles in her home and also patterns on the wall paper and textured ceiling. Sara took photographs of patterns made by railings and shadows. Mazim's picture of the ferry's stern is part of the narrative of his journey, but this photograph reveals a more considered composition. The stern is centered, with a pattern of rails and water on either side. The vertical lines of the railing and the white wake create darker angles at the top corners, suggesting movement. Texture is also suggested by the contrast between the rigid metal rails and the frothy wake. When asked why he took that particular photograph, which he selected as one of his favorites, Mazin did not mention any of these visual features, however, he said "it caught my eye."

Another exceptional photograph is that of a bowl of fruit, taken by Susan who had recently arrived from Uganda. Susan told us that she had arranged the fruit in the colander especially for the photograph, making sure that the word "berries" could be seen. Although she did not say more about her composition, our impression is that she considered color and shape: the circular shapes in contrasting sizes and colors of the apples and grapes are highlighted by the strawberry shape and bright color. The shiny metal bowl is a picture of plenty; it suggests richness and abundance and promises a variety of tastes. The close-up is centered and the lighting makes the fruits' textures come through. This is the most artistic of all the photographs taken by the children and it stands out from the rest of her photographs which were of her sister, herself (including a self-portrait) and her father. Susan said little during the book sessions but would suddenly come up with an insightful comment about an image when the rest of the group had already moved on to the next one. She did not say much about her fruit bowl photograph either, but it is another example of her intelligence and creative potential. She was clearly pleased with the image and the positive comments it evoked from her peers, the teacher, and the researchers.

Visual Journeys Themes

This section describes the features of the photographs in relation to the main themes of the research: journeys, images, and cultural references. It is interesting that two of the children chose to document their journeys: Mazin's trip to Belfast, which we have already discussed, and Sam's daily bus trip to school. As he took photographs from the bus window, Sam, a Scottish boy, seemed to be consciously considering the point of view of a "foreign" spectator of this journey, in portraying his city's landmarks. He said he wanted to show places in Glasgow to people from other countries and he selected the most outstanding buildings he could see on his bus journey: Glasgow University's main building and tower and the Kelvingrove Art Gallery. He also took photographs of other places in the city not from the bus journey, and included some of the city's multicultural aspects. He took photographs of the West End Festival parade which includes people from many different cultures participating, sometimes wearing their traditional costumes. He mentioned that he took the photograph of the Sikh Temple near his house because it is in his country but "it's from another country and other people go there."

There are also cultural references in many of the photographs of the minority ethnic children, particularly Sunil, Samma, Sara, Josef, and Nadia. Sunil took a stunning image of his twin sisters, wearing identical, bright blue, traditional Sri Lankan dresses and jewelry, posing proudly for the camera (a few of the other children also photographed members of their family in traditional dress). Another of his photographs shows a statue of the Virgin Mary in the center, framed by the white angels. Samma photographed Pakistani textiles in her home and both she and Sara took photographs with a reference to religion: a mosque and a prayer rug. Sara also photographed a flag and a framed map of Kurdistan. Among Josef's photographs of single objects are Polish books, including *Harry Potter and the Philosopher's Stone*, board games, and a plate of his favorite food.

Nadia's photographs reflect a Pakistani family culture that now has firm roots in the United Kingdom, but also a hybrid space, with her images of Scottish "lollipop lady" (school crossing attendant) and kitchen staff from school, a Winnie-the-Pooh toy as well as popular Pakistani cultural icons. Images on screen are clearly an important part of Nadia's life. In one photograph her little brother poses next to a large plasma screen TV with a video and digital box. Nadia's obsession with Bollywood, which spilled into her reading and interpretation of the picturebooks, is evident in her photographs: among the 68 photographs, there are 23 of Bollywood stars, all male except one, either from the TV screen or from posters. Several other photographs are of Nadia and her cousins dancing in front of the television showing popular programs. Not all the television screens are Bollywood scenes; there are also British cartoons and an all-female Western pop group.

Images are a significant part of contemporary children's lives, whether they are posters, films, or photographs, and these children chose to tell others about themselves through them. Ali photographed a wall collage of family photos. Morag took one of a billboard advertising the Glasgow 2014 Commonwealth Games. Susan took a picture of a photograph of herself because she liked the way she looked in it, reminding us of the cognitive developmental process described by Sharples et al. (2003) in which photographs allow children to construct and increase control of their identity and, literally in this case, of one's image of oneself.

We would also argue that they increase control of children's own space and the way in which this space, as well as one's identity, is represented to others, all of which are particularly important for newcomers into a culture. Like the children from Hispanic immigrant families in Orellana's study (1999), these children took photos that suggest their participation "in a bicultural world" (80) and that reflect their immigrant community.

Conclusion

Flotsam can act as an incentive for children to reflect on the idea of looking carefully and to think about image construction and about the potential of photography. Smith suggests that in this picturebook it is the boy's ability to actively look beyond the frames (as opposed to the adults in the story who appear distracted by their own concerns) and connect with both the natural world and the imaginary that allow him to find and access the camera's secrets (87). Carrying out visual strategies such as the ones described in this article can help readers to "look beyond the frame" and reflect on constructions of meaning and intervisuality. Dresang and Pantaleo have stressed *Flotsam*'s postmodern "connectivity," a "Radical Change" principle of postmodern picturebooks that according to Pantaleo can refer to "the increased sense of community created [. . .] because form, formats, and subjects encourage sharing among readers" (cited in

Dresang, 45). Pantaleo adds that "the photographs also remind readers of the commonalities and interconnectedness of humans around the world through time" (2008, 27) echoing Wiesner's own description of the camera in *Flotsam* as a way for children to bond with each other, to share a secret "across time and across distance" (2006).

The sharing of the photographs with others can strengthen the community of learners, particularly in an intercultural situation. Speaking about the task, Ms. Finlay, one of the teachers, commented:

> I thought that was a nice idea, to take photos and share this as a little "bit of my life," [such as] the photos of families, because a lot of the times the asylum seekers don't get a chance to do it [. . .] it helped the children learn a lot about each other [something] which they wouldn't have been able to do otherwise; they were [also] very interested in the presentations and enjoyed them.

Photography is a promising way of exploring the visual image, both from an investigative and a pedagogic point of view. As a research method, the main advantage was that it allowed us a glimpse into these children's worlds which would have been difficult to access otherwise. As a pedagogic method, it uses the medium's potential to communicate, narrate or create and draws attention to the metalanguage of image.

In the conclusion of Corona's study (2002) of the Huichol children's photographs, she reflects on how different their photographs are from the clichéd photographs of indigenous peoples usually taken by professional photographers or others.

> The construction of plural society requires that the actors relate to each other without prejudices and free from stigmatizing stereotypes. The possibility of deliberating about our differences [. . .] depends on proper recognition of others. If we accept seeing them as they want to be seen, we have before us an opportunity to relate to our contemporaries in a horizontal manner, in a reciprocal recognition between equals. (63, EA transl.)

For this group of children the photography task became a way of controlling the way they wanted to see and be seen by others, moving away from stereotypes and sharing their wider communities with each other. At the same time the photographs encouraged them to reflect on the idea of looking carefully, increase their understanding of the visual image and to think about artistically complex texts.

References

Arizpe, Evelyn, and Morag Styles. *Children Reading Pictures.* London: RoutledgeFalmer, 2003. Print.

Carranza, Marcela. "*Flotante.*" *Imaginaria* 275 (27 July 2010). Web. 30 Jun. 2011. <http://www.imaginaria.com.ar/2010/07/flotante/>

Corona, Sarah. *Miradas entrevistas: aproximaciones a la cultura, comunicación y la fotografía huichola.* Guadalajara, Jalisco: Universidad de Guadalajara, 2002. Print.

Dresang, Eliza T. "Radical Change Theory, Postmodernism, and Contemporary Picturebooks." *Postmodern Picturebooks.* Ed. Lawrence R. Sipe and Sylvia Pantaleo. London: Routledge, 2008. 41–54. Print.

Evans, Janet. Ed. *Talking Beyond the Page: Reading and Responding to Picturebooks.* London: Routledge, 2009. Print.

Freund, Giselle. *La fotografía como documento social.* Barcelona: Gustavo Gilli, 2006 (1st edition in French 1974). Print.

Moss, Gemma. "Seeing with the Camera: Analysing Children's Photographs of Literacy in the Home." *Journal of Research in Reading* 24.3 (2001): 279–92. Print.

Orellana, Marjorie Faulstich. "Space and Place in an Urban Landscape. Learning from Children's Views of their Social Worlds." *Visual Sociology* 14 (1999): 73–89. Print.

Pantaleo, Sylvia. *Exploring Student's Response to Contemporary Picturebooks.* Toronto: University of Toronto Press, 2008. Print.

—. "The Framed and the Framing in 'Flotsam.'" *Journal of Children's Literature* 34.1 (2008b): 22–29. Print.

Pink, Sara. *Doing Visual Ethnography.* London: Sage, 2007. Print.

Sharples, Mike, Laura Davison, Glyn V. Thomas, and Paul D. Rudman. "Children as Photographers: An Analysis of Children's Photographic Behaviour and Intentions at Three Age Levels." *Visual Communication* 2.3 (2003): 303–30. Print.

Sipe, Lawrence. *Storytime: Young Children's Literary Understanding in the Classroom.* New York: Teachers College Press, 2008. Print.

Smith, Vivienne. "Making and Breaking Frames: Crossing the Borders of Expectation in Picturebooks." *Talking Beyond the Page: Reading and Responding to Picturebooks.* Ed. Janet Evans. London: Routledge, 2009. 81–96. Print.

Wiesner, David. *Flotsam.* New York: Clarion Books, 2006. Print.

—. *Flotsam Logs.* 25 Sept. 2006. Web. 30 Jun. 2011. <http://thefishknowthesecret.com/logs/2006/09/what_is_flotsam_1.html>

—. *The Three Pigs.* New York: Clarion Books, 2002. Print.

—. *Tuesday.* New York: Clarion Books, 1992.

Index

Page numbers in **bold** type refer to figures

Kümmerling-Meibauer, B.: and Meibauer, J. 2, 23–41

La Galera (publisher) 45
La puerta (Van Zeveren) 52
Lambert, S.: and Almond, D. 80
Land of Yellow (Max) 28–9
Landscape with the Fall of Icarus (Brueghel) 18
Larrick, N. 96
Latyk, O. 52
Leafe, M. 101
Lear, E. 11
Lenski, L. 19
Leonhard, L. 25, 29–30
Lepp, M.: and Jersild, P. 72
Leuwen, T. Van: and Kress, G. 125, 128
Licht aus! (Geisert) 52
Limbourg Brothers 13–14, 19
Lindenbaum, P. 70–1, 75–6
Lindgren, A.: and Wikland, I. 77
Lindgren, B.: and Eriksson, E. 75
Lindisfarne Gospels 9
Lionni, L. 50
Lissiat, A.: and Thompson, C. 3, 109–23
literature circles 110
Little Blue and Little Yellow (Lionni) 50
Little Pretty Pocket-Book, A (Newbery) 11
Little Red Riding Hood (Grimm Brothers) 15
Livre de la mer, Le (Baussier) 60
Locke, J. 11
Long Tail Kitty (Pien) 15
Louhi, K. 50
Loup est revenu, Le (De Pennart) 50
Loup, J-J.: and Ruy-Vidal, F. 35
Lucy Brown and Mr Grimes (Ardizzone) 111–12
Lupton, H. 103

Maar, P. 54
McAdam, J.: and Arizpe, E. 3, 141–57; Arizpe, E. and Farrell, M. 1–5
Macaulay, D. 18
McClintock, B. 52
McGuire, C.: and Sipe, L. 43–4
McKean, D.: and Gaiman, N. 78
McKee, D. 76
Madelaine (Bemelman) 67, 72
Madlenka (Sís) 52
Magic in the Mist (Kimmel) 16
Mählqvist, S.: and Nygren, T. 78–80
Maicki Astromaus (Brown) 33
Making Reading Mean (Smith) 111
Mani das lügst du weider (Walbert) 35–6
Manifesto of Surrealism (Breton) 91–2
Manky Mingin Rhymes in Scots (Fitt and Robertson) 102
Manning, M.J. 13
Marantz, K. 7–8

Martin, R. 111–12
Massey, D. 67, 78, 81
Matty's Midnight Monster (Kemp and Timms) 78
Maurer, W. 25, 30–1
Max, P. 25, 28–9
Mayer, M. 72
Maynard, S. 4
Me and My Cat (Kitamura) 76, 80
Meibauer, J.: and Kümmerling-Meibauer, B. 2, 23–41
memory 130–3
Mercer, L. 105
Metzger, D. 110
Middle Ages 9–11
Mikolaycak, C. 103–4
Millions of Cats (Gag) 12
El millor Nadal (Chen) 54
Milne, A.A. 102
Mina (Höglund) 73–4
Mister Bird (Couratin) 31–3
Mitchell, W. 126
Miura, T. 52–4
Moebius, W. 65
Moonlight (Ormerod) 72
Morris, J. 47
Morris, William 42
Mosmann, O. 37
Moss, G. 148–9
Mr Bear (Gliori) 105
Mr Green's Tea (Castán) 50
Müller, G. 60
Munro, M. 101
El muro (Sís) 52
Murphy, J. 70
Museum of Modern Art (New York) 65
Muth, J.: and Charlip, R. 80

New Impulses in Picturebook Research (Kümmerling-Meibauer *et al*) 4
New Review of Children's Literature and Librarianship 1
New York: Museum of Modern Art 65
Newbery, J. (publisher) 11
Newbery, L.: and Rayner, C. 15
Nicholson, W. 12
nightmares 75–9
Nikolajeva, M.: and Scott, C. 8, 26; and Taylor, L. 2, 64–83
Nine Lives of a Cat (Bennett) 11
El niño estrella (Latyk) 52
Nodelman, P. 8, 126–7
Nordqvist, S. 75
Norton, M. 80, 87
Not Now, Bernard (McKee) 76
Nygren, T.: and Mählqvist, S. 78–80
Nyhus, S. 80

INDEX